Dedicated to my father R.L. Singh Yadav for being the pillar of my life and for teaching me to get up and fight back after every failure

THE MOST COMMON MYTHS IN INDIAN FITNESS AND SPORTS SOCIETY

DR. DEV YADAV

Contents

Contents

Foreword

This is a beautiful book about the topic that is directly related to people's misconceptions about sports and fitness. "The most common Myths in Indian Fitness and Sports Society" is a guide for people who have been spreading incorrect information and causing dilemmas in others' minds. Looking into the research material used in the book I am very confident that every person is going to get benefited from reading this. Every topic is described in detail with scientific explanations while keeping it simple. Life is full of myths and legends. There is a myth that lightning never strikes twice in the same spot. Which is not true. Then there's a misconception that tomatoes are a tasty, healthy, nutritious vegetable. In fact, they're classified as a fruit. There are many sports and fitness-related myths that are widely practiced and preached in the sports and fitness world that are just as incorrect as our beliefs about lightning and tomatoes, and in this book, Dr. Dev has cleared many such myths. There is a topic related to the menstruation cycle that is somewhat taboo in India, but this book has elaborated on it very well and made it easier to have a conversation about it in order to bring women to the forefront. This book is not Author's opinion, this is actually based on very deep research. I personally recommend this book to anyone who wants to know the truth about fitness and sports.

Siddhart Srinet

Sports Officer, Government College, Prithvipur, M.P.

B.P.Ed, M.P.Ed, MPhil. NET, Diploma in Coaching (NIS, Patiala)

Preface

"The Most Common Myths in Indian Fitness and Sports Society" is a book dedicated to countering the most common misconceptions about fitness and sports. These misconceptions have stayed in our Indian society for generations and continue to have such a strong influence on our mindset that we have accepted them as truth. This book will assist readers in understanding logically and scientifically the exact truth behind every lie we were told about lifting weights or participating in any sports. In this book, I've discussed the eight most common myths, proven them wrong with evidence, and provided a factual conclusion. I've known many sports professionals, coaches, fitness trainers, and professors carry outdated training and coaching mindsets that are being passed down to the next generation; this book will help us put a stop to it. This book is for anyone who has ever played sports for fun, basic fitness, or professionally. If you have ever done physical fitness or did not do it because of some confusing rumors, this book is for you. This book is for every young athlete's guardian, parents, trainers, and coaches to have a clear idea about the training and its outcome. This book is for any woman who was told not to participate in sports or exercises due to her maturational cycle. This book is written in the service of the nation to promote sports, fitness, and overall well-being.

Preface

Acknowledgements

I'd like to express my gratitude to everyone who helped me to finish this book in any way. First and foremost, I thank Goddess for providing me with the strength and knowledge to complete this task.

I am grateful to Mr. K. Krishnam Raju for discussing and motivating me to write on this particular matter for which I am deeply thankful.

I am also thankful to Nikhil Gautam, Jai Prakash Singh, Dev Singh, and Siddharth Srinet for their support and friendship.

My thanks to my trainees Isha Raju, Veda Raju, and Muthyala Vineeth for encouraging me to finish the book as soon as possible.

My sincere thanks to my Mentor Dr. M. Stalin Nagarajan for showing trust and faith in me.

Finally, I'd like to convey my gratefulness for my family's support and love. My parents, R.L. Singh Yadav and Sharada Devi Yadav, and My sister, Suman Yadav, and brother Shailendra Yadav. They were all essential in sustaining my motivation.

Disclamer

"The information in this book is not intended to replace medical advice, emergency treatment, or proper first-aid training, Don't use this information to diagnose or formulate a treatment plan for a health condition or disease without consulting a qualified health care specialist. Although it is aimed to give accurate information on the subject matter addressed; however, it is not intended to substitute direct expert guidance. If this level of assistance is required, a qualified professional should be contacted."

Introduction

"The Most Common Myths in Indian Fitness and Sports Society" is written to lead readers to the truth about sports and fitness myths. Many times, we are discouraged from participating in sports or other forms of physical activity due to a lack of knowledge or a misunderstanding about the outcome. This book will help you understand the subject matter scientifically and clearly. There are eight chapters in this book, and each chapter discusses one misconception and then elaborates on it neatly to help the reader understand the actual facts behind it. There are numerous misconceptions that exist in the Indian fitness and sporting field, as well as in the general public's mind, one of them is that height growth is affected by strength training at a young age. Strength training should not be introduced to a child before the age of fourteen, according to popular belief. Many sports professionals and fitness trainers can be heard saying that you should not take your child to physical training that includes strength training activity, and many well-educated people agree with them. Because of this, many young professional players who aspire to be elite athletes are not exposed to strength training by their coaches. Some people believe that excessive physical activity, such as sports, can stunt a child's growth. Many of you are already aware of the truth behind this concept, but this book will assist you in explaining it in depth using scientific explanations; now, let's go and read everything in detail.

Introduction

ONE

MYTH -1- STRENGTH TRAINING AT AN EARLY AGE STUNTS HEIGHT

There are an anonymous number of misconceptions that live in the Indian fitness and sporting industry as well as in the common mindset, but the biggest misconception is about height growth affected by strength training at an early age remains on the top. Commonly it is believed that no strength training should be introduced to a child before the age of fourteen. Many sports professionals and fitness trainers can also be heard saying that do not take your son or daughter to physical training which involves strength training activity, you can also find many highly educated people agreeing with it. A high number of young professional players who wants to become elite athlete are not exposed to strength training by their coaches due to believing that it might stunt or inhibits their growth. Some also believe that intense physical activity through sports may stunt a child's growth. People might see people who lift weights that are short and stocky and also some successful and popular gymnasts are not very tall in heights and they start believing that they did not grow tall because of their heavy lifting gym sessions.

This common belief has zero evidence to support it. Many studies have looked at this exact topic and found out that strength training has no negative impact on skeletal growth or in common language it does not stunt (stop) the height of a child because of early age strength training. Instead, the research suggests that when strength training is programmed appropriately and performed with good technique and appropriate posture that it provides numerous benefits for young athletes. Some of these benefits include increased strength, speed, and power, improved body composition, stronger and healthier bones, and better balance and stability.

The first thing I would like to address is that no studies have ever shown that lifting weights stunts or inhibits growth. But, as with any exercise program, if you do too much too soon, physical problems like sprain, and strain can occur no matter how old the person doing the exercise is. The most important aspects when training as a child or teen is supervision, exercise technique, lightweight, and high repetitions in the 12, 15, and even 20 reps range. As a teen, you may gradually progress to heavier weights with lower reps, around 10 reps per set. Once a teen player or a teen fitness enthusiast gets used to a particular load and gets the posture right during the exercise overall progressive load can be applied also starting with own body weight, bands, dumbbells, and the barbell are safer than directly jumping on machines to avoid injuries. As with any exercise program, supervision is the key. The risk of injury is always there but it can be avoided by proper technique and supervision. Some common injuries in children from weight lifting include fractures, spondylolysis, meniscal tears, and herniated disks. Most of these injuries happen because a child is working out on his/her own without any proper guidance and supervision. For healthy children and young sportsmen who are taught proper lifting forms by qualified trainers and who work out in a supervised, non-competitive to moderate competitive environment, the risk of injury is very low and the potential for benefits is great. Motivation is another biggest aspect of a great outcome but A child being pushed by an aggressive coach or high expecting parent should not be training. A serious young athlete with reasonable training goals, supportive parents, and a qualified coach can achieve the most from strength training.

The teen should follow a general strengthening program that offers age-appropriate exercises and teaches proper movement patterns, while also targeting major muscle groups, including the core. Fitness programs should also include cardio exercises that are good for the heart, such as biking and running, as well as exercises that increase flexibility, such as foam rolling and static or dynamic flexibility sessions.

A young sportsman should be following a well-designed strength and conditioning program which supports their game and the nature of particular sports. Different sports have different kind of strength requirement which is very specific to that particular game and sports. To make your workouts as efficient as possible, you should choose compound exercises. Compound exercises are those which involve more than one joint movement. A strength training program for young athletes should address every major muscle group in the body. A comprehensive strength training program should target all major muscle groups in the body, including the chest, upper back, shoulders, biceps, triceps, neck (for collision sports), abdominals, lower back, hips, glutes, quadriceps, hamstrings, and calves. Some sports may focus on one body part or require special attention to smaller muscle groups (e.g., bawlers in cricket will train the shoulder muscles extensively), but all major muscle groups need to be trained. It is recommended to perform equal amounts of work on both sides of a joint.

Another point we need to understand is the difference between strength training and weight training or weight lifting, right now we need to understand muscular strength. Muscular strength is defined as the ability to exert force against resistance. Besides enabling us to overcome resistance, muscle strength also determines our stability, reduces injury risk, and increases bone density to name a few.

What is Strength Training?

The term strength training refers to any exercise that uses some form of resistance to strengthen and build muscle. You can create that resistance by using hand-held weights, weight machines, and resistance bands also Pilates and yoga classes are examples of strength-training workouts that use just your body weight to strengthen muscles. In simple words, Strength training is a term that is used to refer to any kind of training that helps in building strength.

What is weight training?

Weight training or weight lifting is a type of strength training that specifically includes the use of weights to build muscle and improve strength, Weight training involves the use of a variety of sizes and shapes of weights according to one's needs and requirements to strengthen and construct muscles. Weight training is mainly categorized into two broad types free weights and machines. You can use free weights or machines to train specific muscles or in general for working out. In modern sports training weight lifting is one of the most common ways to train strength.

As we are clear about strength training and weight training or weight lifting, let us be sure that any kind of strength training or weight lifting does not have any negative impact on the height growth of children, despite it helps them to improve bone density, tendon, and ligament strength, helping athletes prepare for the physical demands of the sport. So before making up our minds and thinking that weight lifting can affect the height growth of a person, we need to understand what exactly determines height.

What factors determine human height?

Researchers estimate that about 80 percent of an individual's height is determined by the **DNA** sequence variants they inherit. Before assuming a person will be the same height as their parents, there are many factors to consider. Medical conditions, hormonal deficiencies, environment, and more can all affect your height. Sometimes height can be predicted depending on how tall or short your parents are, you'll end up somewhere between their average heights. But there is another factor that should be considered that DNA is passed down to the next generation in big slabs called chromosomes. Every generation, each parent passes half their chromosomes to their child and the odds are pretty high that you have DNA from your great, great, great grandparent. The genetics of height Genes aren't the sole predictor of a person's height. In some instances, a child might be much taller than their parents and other relatives. Or, perhaps, they may be much shorter. A person's height is influenced by a variety of factors other than genetics, especially during childhood and adolescence.

Hormones are one of the major factors for height development. During puberty, hormones are essential for regulating body growth. These include thyroid hormones, human growth hormones, and gender determining hormones such as testosterone and estrogen. A malfunction in these hormones could affect your growth as well as your height. If a child develops hypothyroidism (low thyroid) or pituitary gland disorders, their height may be shorter than their parents. A person's height can be influenced by certain conditions present at birth. Achondroplasia (dwarfism), for example, is a rare bone growth disorder that tends to run in families. Short stature can also result from Turner syndrome, another congenital disorder, it causes delayed puberty. Turner syndrome is not hereditary like achondroplasia. Marfan syndrome and Klinefelter syndrome are other congenital conditions resulting in taller than normal stature. Marfan syndrome is caused by enlargements of connective tissue. Klinefelter syndrome occurs when a male is born with an additional copy of the X chromosome.

Nutrition is one of the aspects which determines the height of a person. Human growth and development, including height, depend on an adequate supply of nutrition during the growing years. You can achieve your genetic height potential by eating whole, nutritious foods, on the other hand, a poor diet can lead to a shorter stature compared to your parents.

The environment is another which may affect teens' height growth, many young kids in India are still working in unsafe factories, less equipped restaurants kitchens, and small workshops and warehouses, where proper sunlight and healthy oxygen are not available and they lack nutritional food as well, which affects their overall growth and development and height growth could be one of it.

Gender is another aspect that determines the height growth of a person, most people gain about 2 inches in height each year between the ages of one and puberty. When you reach puberty, you may grow at a rate of 4 inches per year. Everyone, however, develops at a different rate. This growth spurt typically begins in the early adolescent years for girls. Boys may not notice this sudden increase in height until they are in their late teens. When a child reaches puberty, usually stops growing taller. This means that as an adult, you are unlikely to grow taller.

As we looked into every aspect which affects height, now it's safe to say that there is no negative effect of weight lifting or strength training at an early age or teenager Lifting weights during puberty or your adolescent years does not affect your height. Because weight training is directly related to increased testosterone production, it may help your muscles grow bigger, denser, and stronger, as well as taller. As previously stated, certain activities, such as weight lifting, will not stunt your growth. Exercise causes the release of HGH, which aids in growth. Exercise and weight lifting during puberty are beneficial because they can prepare you to be much stronger and healthier throughout your life. So it is clear that strength training will not prevent growth unless you have an injury to your epiphyseal growth plate (The epiphyseal growth plate consists of a layer of cartilage present only during the growth period and vanishes soon after puberty in long bones, situated at each end of a long bone.) Children as young as seven years old can begin strength training if they can understand the instructions.

You only need to focus on the form and technique of the exercises. As a result, it is preferable, to begin with, light or no weight and gradually increase the weight once you have learned the technique completely. Youth athletes and nonathletes alike can successfully and safely improve their strength and overall health by participating in a well-supervised strength training program. Trained fitness professionals play an essential role in ensuring proper technique, form, progression of exercises, and safety in this age group. Strengthening exercises have many advantages. It reinforces your muscles and bones, assists you with keeping a solid weight, and advances HGH creation. Youngsters in school ought to get an hour of activity daily. During this time, they should zero in on strength-building workouts, like push-ups or sit-ups, adaptability works out, like yoga vigorous exercises, like playing tag, working out with a rope, or trekking and other team and individual games and sports. Exercising as an adult has its benefits, too. additionally, to help you maintain your overall health, it also can help reduce your risk of osteoporosis. This condition occurs when your bones become weak or brittle, leading to bone density loss. this will cause you to "shrink." To reduce your risk, try walking, playing tennis, or practicing yoga several times every week. Doing yoga along with a strengthening program can help a young athlete or non-athlete in maintaining the right body posture as well as injury prevention. Yoga practice can strengthen your muscles, align your body, and help together with your posture. this may assist you to stand taller. You can practice yoga within the comfort of your house or in a group setting at your local gym or studio.

So, the bottom line is that strength training, weight training, or weight lifting does not stunt or inhibit height growth. There is no scientific evidence supporting the fact that lifting weights will have any negative effect on your height when performed properly.

TWO

MYTH -2- WOMEN SHOULDN'T LIFT HEAVY BECAUSE IT'S DANGEROUS

Another misleading belief is that Women should not be lifting heavy as men as it's dangerous and they might end up injuring them. But facts are completely against this belief too. Weight lifting is a sport where women are capable of excelling. While heavy weight lifting is commonly labeled as a sport for men, women athletes are among the strongest on earth. In terms of strength relative to their body weight, women weight lifters may be able to outlift men, regardless of their total weight. Furthermore, weight lifting is not harmful to women, even if they are not athletes. Any activity is dangerous if done incorrectly.

Lifting weights with proper form is completely safe. Women of all ages and backgrounds can safely learn and practice weight lifting under supervision. Recent research shows that pregnant women can even lift weights safely - but only if they have prior experience.

Compared with other common sports such as basketball, football, and running, weight lifting sports like powerlifting and CrossFit have a relatively low injury rate. It is widely assumed that if you want to look better, you should tone your muscles without bulking them up. The idea is that there are specific types of workouts that will help you achieve this, usually involving a lot of repetition with light weights, but this is not a realistic or healthy way to look at your muscles. Your muscle will still not grow if they are not being challenged in every workout session. If your muscles don't grow on their own, they won't look any different than they do presently, even if you can somehow get rid of the fat on your body. Another way to put it is that your body will not look healthy and fit until its muscle tissues are well-trained, whether you have excess fat or not. Another common term is shaping the muscle, but the truth is that you cannot shape a muscle because it is already in a shape determined by your genetics. However, if you are a talented bodybuilder, you can change their size in proportion to the size of nearby muscles and you can certainly reshape your body by making some muscles bigger and some muscles smaller to give a more proportionate look. Sculpting is the term I prefer to use instead of toning or shaping. It refers to a combination of muscle gain and fat loss that leaves the lifter's physics looking sculpted. However, you can't sculpt your muscle until you've built it.

A simple point to remember is that a muscle fiber in a woman is structurally identical to a muscle fiber in a man. There are some chemical differences due to the need to interact with different hormones at the cell membrane level but these differences do not affect the functional abilities of muscle. Women may have different genders, but they are not different species.

If you have a regular workout schedule and are now ready to take on a bigger challenge as a woman. Perhaps you've been working out for a while but haven't made much progress recently because you're afraid of injuring yourself, or perhaps you've never done weight training before and would like to learn how to do it correctly from the start. When it comes to strength training, I'm here to help and guide you on how to develop a stronger and tighter body, a great figure, and boost your self-confidence. Strength training is all about daring to be better and pushing yourself a little bit further because of the numerous benefits you will reap. Weight training strengthens the skeleton system, stimulates weight loss, reduces the risk of injury, increases stamina, and improves sleep quality. In other words, you will have more energy to do your daily tasks, carry your groceries, have a better appearance, and respond positively. If you are an athlete, your performance will be much more economical, less tiring, and less harmful. Many women are concerned about getting back into shape after giving birth because they feel mentally weaker than physically, but it is important to understand that weight training not only changes you physically but also allows you to evolve mentally. You push, you hold, you expel every ounce of energy from your muscles, and you feel like a champion. So welcome to the exciting world of strength training, where results are guaranteed if you don't skip any of the steps, do not take a break from the program routine, make the best of what you have, push yourself hard, and enjoy your success.

Women who are fully engaged in midlife and try to become fit by focusing on weight loss, whether through planned diets, excessive exercise, or both, often experience an increased level of stress. They believe they have made poor nutritional choices, and they have disrupted sleep patterns, impaired immunity, slower metabolism, and hormonal disturbances, all of which can hinder successful weight loss, weight maintenance, or muscle building. Strength training, on the other hand, makes it easier to get fit and trim in a sustainable and healthy manner. And it's never too late to begin; you can build muscles at any age, lose weight at any age, and become stronger and more energetic whether you're twenty-five, forty-five, or seventy years old; all you have to do is put in the effort. Physical activity and proper nutrition are required for good results. This is not something you can do in the heat of the moment; you must make a concerted effort and focus on every workout and meal. You will train more intensely than ever before, sweating and feeling out of breath. You won't be lifting dumbbells while planning your dinner, neither you'll exercise with the intention of changing how you look and feel. You will need to set aside some time for this. Depending on where you are now, your diet may need to be modified or completely changed. Because building a strong and beautiful body is as much about nutrition as it is about exercise, each step has a dietary component. Fitness, in my opinion, is more of a mental challenge than a physical one. Because everything begins in your mind, if you want to achieve something and are willing to put in the effort, you will be able to make it happen. It must be crystal clear to you that the outcome is entirely dependent on your effort and work. You get what you put into it, so if you train well, eat properly, and stick to the program, the results are guaranteed, and you will succeed. Schedule your workout for the time of day when you feel the most energized to make it easier and more enjoyable. Having a partner who shares your goals could be beneficial. Follow the same diet and go through the plan together. If things get tough, you two can lean on each other. Consider your motivation for pursuing this training. Why do you want to begin this program? Is it to become more powerful? Is it to feel better or to look better? Whatever your reasons are, they must be your own; they cannot be those of your neighbors, friends, or spouse. Finally, prioritize your commitment and take it seriously; this is about you, your health, and your well-being. You want to be comfortable in your own skin. This is time well spent. Let us now discuss a safe and appropriate program for women. It is entirely up to you whether you exercise at home or in a gym. You won't be able to use your lack of time to go to the gym as an excuse because you can work out in your living room. If you prefer to work out at home, that's fine, but you must use weights that allow you to complete optimum reps and are heavy enough to test your strength. The most significant disadvantage of working out at home is that you must invest in proper equipment.

Some do not believe this and think that 11 to 12 pounds of weight or 5 to 10 kgs of weight is more than adequate for the job. That may be true for a short time, but your workout will quickly become ineffective as it becomes too light for you. Proper weights are necessary tools for achieving good results. Women typically have less upper body strength and more lower body strength, so if you want to combine gym and home workout sessions, train your upper body at home and your lower body at the gym where you'll have access to heavier weights. If you have the option of using free weights like dumbbells and barbells or machines, always go with the free weights. When you're stuck in a single position with a machine, there's no way to naturally balance and stabilize your body as you would do with free weights. Machine exercises are difficult to isolate, and our design focuses on only one muscle or muscle group at a time. However, if you use free weights, you will be working on the muscles from different angles while also possibly with the help of other muscles. Including an aerobic workout in the program is beneficial if done for a specific period of time twice a week. If you are looking for solid gain strength, you will not get it from participating in an aerobics class because there are too many restrictions for exercise, and the tempo is too fast, which means you don't have enough time to stretch the muscle to its fullest extent, and your form suffers as a result. When it comes to strength training, form comes first. If you are a beginner, a training class may help you at first, but after a while, you will hit a plateau and your progress will slow down. Always adjust your exercise routine to fit your capabilities in terms of rest periods, peace, and the amount of weight you need to use for the best results. Measuring your progress is critical when following a strength training program. Taking pictures and creating a timeline can be motivating to track your progress. Another way to take record video and see how everything looks and feels. It is critical to track your results in order to demonstrate that you have made progress with this program. Progress pictures, scale weighing, tape measurements, and skinfold caliper measurements are examples of these measurements. I recommend beginning with what you are most comfortable with and gradually increasing your comfort level. The more data you have on yourself, the better you will be able to experiment with variables such as increasing reps, sets, or weight used during workouts, increasing the number of hours you sleep each night, increasing the amount of cardio you do each week, and/or increasing or decreasing the number of calories you eat each day.

It is entirely up to you how frequently you measure your progress, but I would recommend doing so once a month or every six weeks to ensure consistency.

How women should perform strength training with safety?

It is important to realize that each body has a unique starting point and understanding of strength training standards and best practices. Many people are not aware of the science behind strength training. The following strength training principles must be included in these discussions as educational topics for better results and safety.

Weight Size & Overload

A new strength training practitioner must understand when and how to increase the weights and how to progress with weight size over time. It is critical to understand the value of observation in making these assessments. For example, a person should notice if they do not feel fatigued at the end of an exercise set with proper form (and can easily do 5-6 more repetitions) or if the workout routine does not challenge them, it might mean that they are not using the most appropriate weight size and incorporate the fitness principle of progressive overload. According to the fitness principle of progressive overload, we must overload the neuromuscular systems over time in order to create and sustain physiological adaptations from strength training. On a similar note, when we strength train, we break down muscle fibers and attempt to overload this system to rebuild them stronger. Keeping this goal in mind it is advantageous to be fatigued by the last repetition of an exercise set (with proper form), to be able to move less weight, and to complete fewer repetitions at the end of a workout.

It is best if you understand that when you use the appropriate weight size and challenge yourself in the workout, you will most likely not be able to train at the same intensity or with the same load that you started with at the start of the exercise session. Overloading the neuromuscular system with the appropriate weight size over time allows the body to adapt and rebuild stronger.

Progression

It is critical to understand progression, which states that no more than 10% of training time, distance covered, or weight used in a given exercise or activity should be increased each week. Following the 10% rule allows for gradual body adaptations and reduces the risk of overuse injuries. Train with this 10% rule in mind, and don't be afraid to lift heavier weights. As recommended. Understand the significance of not sacrificing proper exercise form for an increase in weight size. Speed and load are less important than form. It is useful to know that if you are unsure whether you should increase by 10%, start with a 5% increase and reconsider from there. What to do when you are between weight sizes on a specific exercise is another useful tip to share with new strength training practitioners. Individuals who are new to strength training often do not realize that if they become fatigued in the middle of an exercise set and are unable to complete any more repetitions, they can quickly grab lighter weights to complete their final repetitions. This will provide you with additional advantages for your strength and endurance goals. Using this tip when needed will eventually help you get stronger and complete a full set with heavier loads. These informational tips may seem obvious to fitness professionals, but they can make all the difference for those who are new to strength training in general.

Principle Of Specificity

The principle of specificity is another important concept to grasp. According to the fitness principle of specificity, the body's adaptation or change in physical fitness is specific to the type of training performed. In other words, as you practice, you will become more skilled at what you do. It can be explained in terms of strength training as individuals continue improving what they train for. For instance, if you want to master push-ups, you have to work your chest, core, and arms. If you want to run faster in a race, train for that if you want big biceps, you should be training your biceps if you want strong legs to have to work on that. Let me elaborate that how you can get better at push-ups? The answer is frequently to keep practicing and do more push-ups because doing so will help the body adapt to handle more repetitions and load for that exercise. Other pectoral strength exercises can help increase overall muscular endurance and strength. However, to improve at a specific movement pattern or exercise, you must keep practicing and refine that movement pattern or exercise. For example, if a person wants to improve and train their body to run more, they must run. Coaches and trainers must educate those who are new to strength training on the importance of not skipping or eliminating what may be difficult for them. What is difficult for a person may be a sign that it is exactly what he or she requires to grow stronger. As fitness professionals or athletes from other sports who train their strength, it is critical to understand the significance of specifying what they want to improve in strength training. Similarly, emphasize the importance of not pushing through pain while doing what is difficult.

Rest & Recovery

Our muscles have an ideal training duration length-tension relationship. Muscles that are either overly long and stretched or overly tight and strong can cause physical pain and injury.

That is why incorporating active recovery techniques, workouts, and rest days, such as dynamic and passive flexibility, into a weekly strength training and fitness program is critical. As fitness professionals, Coaches and trainers, we must educate our players and clients on the value of rest and recovery in achieving their goals. Make an effort to educate on this subject to reduce over-exercise and avoidable injuries from overuse. Inform players and clients that rest and recovery are where the majority of physiological adaptations from strength training occur and are frequently the missing link in many fitness programs. Before it is too late, it is critical to explain the relationship between rest and progress, as well as the relationship between lack of rest and the possibility of injury. Everyone needs to understand that rest and recovery are beyond passive static stretches, dynamic mobility work, and foam rolling exercises. Rest and recovery also imply getting enough sleep and eating properly. A good night's sleep of 7-9 hours per night is essential for the recovery process. Taking a day off from weight training, using self-myofascial release, and prioritizing dynamic mobility and passive stretching every week are also critical. For greater outcomes, understand the importance of diet and hydration before beginning or upgrading a strength training program.

Frequency

Frequency refers to how often you should work out. If you want to improve at something or reach a goal, you must keep practicing frequently and consistently. Make a schedule to commit to a certain number of recurring workouts per week. Follow it regularly and for longer periods of time. When discussing workouts, intensity refers to performing an exercise with such intensity that it becomes extremely difficult to complete, with the last three repetitions being close to the maximum effort you can manage. It is the push to muscle failure if you are strength training or running intervals. Maintain a lively workout with a high level of intensity. Increase the difficulty once you're confident in your form. Don't sit when you can stand, use free weights instead of machines, and focus on basic moves rather than isolation exercises.

Nutrition & Hydration

It is essential to understand the requirements for pre-, during-, and post-workout hydration. There are strategies provided to assist these recommendations to an individual in particular. Still, for general guidance, one should drink at least 20 ounces about 60-90 minutes before a workout, 4-6 ounces every 15 minutes during the workout, and 16-24 ounces after a workout. It is crucial to understand the nutritional significance of pre and post-workout fuel. It is the responsibility of fitness professionals, coaches, and trainers to communicate the importance of eating a healthy meal at least two hours before a workout. Furthermore, if they haven't had a proper meal, explain how they can benefit from eating a healthy snack about 30 minutes before a strength training session. Talk about what they need to do post-workout, in addition to pre-workout, to help them jump-start the recovery process. Everyone should be aware that a healthy snack containing lean protein and complex carbohydrates should be consumed within a 30–45-minute window following a workout. They should also be made aware that the sooner they do this, the better their body and recovery will be.

It's also important to understand why you need to eat in such a specific way, as well as how getting enough protein aids tissue repair, and getting enough of the right type of carbohydrates can help maximize the recovery process and replace energy stores.

Along with following the principles of strength training, proper nutrition, and warm-up schedule one should be having proper training gear when it comes to safety, let's discuss what weight lifting accessories are required for both men and women to have safe and comfortable workouts.

1. **Weight Training Shoes**

Many girls and boys are seen lifting weights in sandals and slippers, which is very very dangerous. In some professional gyms, inappropriate footwear is even prohibited. The reason is straightforward. It is dangerous, and you can easily injure yourself while lifting or dropping something on your foot. You should wear sturdy, well-cushioned shoes. They are also ergonomically designed to protect your ankle, feet, and toes. They also support your joints and assist you in maintaining your balance while lifting. Some shoes are designed specifically for powerlifters to provide additional protection and safety. Get one of those if at all possible. You will not regret it since they will also help to lift heavier weights.

2-Towel-

Take a towel and wipe down your body and the equipment you're using. But remember to bring a clean one each time because it will be stinky after a sweaty workout.

3-Weight lifting belt

When performing exercises with heavy weights, it is critical to strengthen your core to handle the weight. This is especially true when performing leg or full-body movements like squats, deadlifts, or sumo lifts. Your lower back will benefit from additional support from the weightlifting belt, but wearing a lifting belt is only necessary if you want to push yourself and lift weights that are exceptionally heavy for you. Most of the time, you don't need to use weights for 6 or more reps or general strength training.

4- Training Gloves

When working out with resistance weights, the bars or dumbbells frequently rub against your skin. This can harden the skin and cause peeling on your hands. It can be difficult to remove, but it is also noticeable when someone clasps your hand. It might not be such a big deal for men. However, for women knowing that their hands will not feel soft and feminine may affect their confidence, which a pair of gym gloves can help to prevent. Weight lifting gloves are typically thickly padded on the palm, and the tops of the fingers are cut off for better grabbing. Weight lifting pads are an alternative to gloves. These pads are typically constructed of spongy or rubber materials. They should be worn on your palms and may provide better control than gloves because a larger portion of your hand is in contact with the bar.

5- Wrist Straps-

Another common problem with weightlifting is the effect it has on the joints. Injuries are caused by lifting heavy weights and using incorrect forms. One way to avoid this is to invest in wrist straps, which help to protect wrist joint movement while performing the exercises.

6-Lifting straps-

Another point of debate in the bodybuilding and fitness community is whether or not to use lifting straps. It has both advantages and disadvantages. The main advantage of using a strap is that you can lift heavy weights without worrying about the bar slipping. As a result, you can gain muscle mass and strength. The obvious disadvantage is that your grips and forearm will not develop "naturally." In general, it is not necessary to use it all of the time. However, if you do, devote some time to strengthening your forearms and grip.

7-Knee Wraps or Sleeves

Knee wraps or sleeves provide additional benefits such as knee pain relief, reduced knee joint inflammation, and reduced swelling when used correctly and sparingly. It is critical to understand that knee wraps or sleeves are intended to enhance and support heavy lifting. So, if your squat form is poor and you have pre-existing joint issues, knee wraps may not be very beneficial.

In conclusion, it is safe to say that any woman in a common or female athlete who is supervised during weight training sessions, guided properly well-equipped, and follows principles of strength training can lift as heavy as men without getting any injury and can achieve her training goals.

THREE

MYTH -3- WOMEN WILL BULK UP IF THEY DO WEIGHT LIFTING

The women's weightlifting revolution has picked up steam in the western world. Women are picking up barbells and dumbbells in growing numbers, gaining their strength and power, and doing better in sports competitions and in daily life as well. Despite its growing popularity, there are still a lot of people in India who believe that "weightlifting will make women bulky and masculine.". Lifting heavy weights as a woman will not make you bulky, manly, or masculine. It will do the opposite: it will tighten and tone your entire body, burn fat, and shape you up. Further in this chapter, we are going to understand why a woman can't bulk up even if she lifts heavy weights in the gym 6 days a week for years and years. As you begin work on your muscle-building journey, keep in mind that building muscle has numerous advantages for women. It not only increases your metabolism, transforming your body into a more efficient fat-burning machine, but it also improves your self-esteem. When you walk into a room, you will stand taller and feel more confident about yourself. Strength training has also been shown to slow bone loss, lowering the risk of osteoporosis-related fractures. If you're worried about bulking up, don't bother because women's testosterone levels are approximately 20% lower than men's, which means that if you want to make your biceps and triceps big, you'll need to massively raise your calorie intake and target workouts and still there will be no bulking up as there is significantly less testosterone in women in comparison to men which is a major muscle-building hormone. Don't think that just because you lift heavy and exercise hard that you'll end up looking like a professional woman bodybuilder because 99.9% of the time, you won't. Remaining a natural athlete while utilizing a healthy, nutrient-dense diet, proper supplementation, proper exercise programs, and recovery techniques are how you achieve a lean, firm, tight, athletic body.

If body fat is a concern, weight training can also help with weight loss. Usually, burning calories is associated with a cardio workout. However, muscle burns more calories than body fat—even when you are at rest. This helps create a calorie deficit, leading to greater fat loss. This can leave you with increased confidence, cognitive clarity, elevated mood, attractive curves, and a new outlook in the weight room.

Testosterone and bulking

The two major hormones involved in lean muscle development are testosterone and the human growth hormone. Everyone has both, but men have significantly more testosterone than women. In general, women have a 15-20% lower testosterone concentration in their bodies than men.

Does weight lifting increase testosterone in women? Maybe, but not by much. According to one study, serum testosterone levels in men only increased significantly after strength training. And it only increased significantly when the weight used in the training was heavier. The bottom line is as follows. Women simply cannot as in they are biologically unable to build large muscles like men without that extra testosterone. This is supported by science. So it's time to stop worrying about gaining too much muscle mass while weight training. For example, lifting heavy, boosts serum testosterone concentration, according to the study. Following a heavy resistance training session, T levels rise in both genders. However, due to women's genetic makeup, females are unable to build the type of muscle that men do.

Anabolic-Androgenic Steroids

Males use testosterone to achieve higher levels of muscle gain. Females cannot grow muscle tissue to the same extent as men because their testosterone levels are lower. They also have higher estrogen and progesterone levels. And then, the question arises What About Female Bodybuilders? Isn't this an example of heavy weightlifting leading to bulk?

The majority of these examples are of professional female bodybuilders. However, women's muscle size is not obtained solely through lifting. Many professional female bodybuilders use anabolic-androgenic steroids, testosterone, and other ergogenic aids to achieve a physique worthy of the title. According to research, using these substances can help increase muscle mass and strength much faster than natural means. Yes, some women can build large muscles. But achieving that level of lean mass does not come from simply lifting heavy weights. Sports scientists have known for a long time that different training protocols can be used to manipulate the body's hormonal response of course to an extent.

In the 1930s, anabolic steroids were discovered to promote muscle growth and improve athletic performance. These substances have been used by bodybuilders, athletes, and others to improve performance and cosmetic appearance since the 1950s. The International Olympic Committee first prohibited the use of anabolic steroids in 1975. Most athletic organizations now prohibit the use of these substances, and drug testing in professional sports has become commonplace. Because of the growing public awareness of steroid abuse, these substances are now regulated by the federal government. Anabolic steroids were classified as schedule III controlled substances for the first time in 1990, and a new law expanded the definition of anabolic steroids in 2004 to include substances that could be converted to testosterone, such as androstenedione. Current clinical applications of these substances in women include libido disorders, cachexia caused by chronic diseases such as HIV, and anemia. Clinical use necessitates a prescription from a licensed physician as well as close monitoring.

Anabolic-androgenic steroids (AAS) are testosterone derivatives that maximize anabolic effects while minimizing androgenic effects. Exogenous testosterone is rapidly degraded and does not affect performance. Men have traditionally used AAS to gain muscle. AAS has also been used by women to increase strength and lean muscle mass. When East German athletes routinely received steroids from team doctors, the use of AAS by women became widely publicized and was known by the world. Rather being a negative impact on health it has become extremely popular amongst athletes and bodybuilders.

Women who use AAS may experience androgenic side effects such as deepening of the voice, acne, male pattern baldness, menstrual irregularities, and increased facial hair. A survey of steroid-using female bodybuilders found that 64% reported an adverse psychological effect, most commonly fragile mood, irritability, or aggressive behavior. Liver damage is one of the more serious side effects. There have been temporary increases in hepatic enzymes that return to normal after steroids are stopped. Steroids were designated as a Schedule III controlled substance under the Anabolic Steroid Control Act of 1990. AAS are prohibited for any purpose other than disease treatment, according to the 1988 Anti-Drug Abuse Act. Steroids are also prohibited by all major sports leagues.

let's try to understand what takes to build muscle in men or women. There are lots of things you have to do to maximize muscle growth during a bulk; the idea that you can gain muscle "fast" naturally can be misleading to those who believe they can build a lot of muscle in one month. The harsh reality is that muscle growth is significantly slower than fat gain, which is why, if you want to maximize muscle growth while minimizing fat gain during a bulk, you must keep track of your nutrition and training every week.

Calories Surplus

Muscle can build, but it takes time and consistency to achieve a decent bulk. During a bulk, however, things such as eating more calories than you burn, increasing protein/

carb intake, training with increased volume, and keeping track of your weight gain will help you create more muscle. To gain muscle and weight during a bulk, you must consume more calories than you burn. It's a simple math equation that has been proven. You must be in a caloric surplus to gain weight and you must be in a caloric deficit to lose weight. Eating whatever you want is one way to accomplish this; however, it may affect the composition of the weight you are gaining and how fast you are gaining weight. As previously stated, you want to ensure that you are eating at a rate that allows for maximum muscle growth while preventing excessive body fat gain during the bulk. You will gain some body fat, but gaining too much will not help you gain more muscle, and may even make your body more likely to prioritize fat gain over muscle gain as your bulk progresses. The key here is to gradually increase your caloric intake rather than eating everything in sight right away. This allows you to ensure that you are tracking your weight gain rate and maximizing your muscle growth to fat gain ratio.

Right Nutrition

Proteins-

If you consume enough calories, you will almost certainly consume enough protein. However, it is critical to consume enough protein to support muscle recovery and growth. During your bulk, aim for 0.8-1.0 grams of protein per pound of body weight. Consuming less protein may result in less muscle growth and recovery. More protein may or may not be necessary because your body can only use so much protein. If you find yourself eating an excessive amount of protein, replace it with more carbohydrates, as carbohydrates are the preferred fuel source for your muscles. Protein can be found in a variety of foods, including meats, legumes, and some cereal products. Proteins in your body serve a variety of functions, including serving as an energy source. They also play an important structural role in many parts of your body, including muscle, bone, and skin. Proteins enable us to move, collaborate with our immune systems to keep us healthy, and regulate numerous chemical reactions required for life. Steak, chicken, whole eggs, turkey, fish, pork, beans, protein powder, dairy products, and lean ground meats are the best sources. Choose tofu, seeds, quinoa, beans, and non-dairy protein powders if you're vegan.

Carbohydrates-

Carbohydrates are the preferred fuel for muscle and brain tissue. While fats and protein can provide energy to the brain, muscles, and body, carbohydrates are the preferred source of energy to allow for high-intensity weight training, the type of training that you will need to be doing to maximize muscle growth. Begin with 2-3 grams of carbs per pound of body weight and gradually increase this macronutrient to match increases in overall calorie intake. Carbohydrates can be found in a variety of foods, including rice and pasta, as well as fruits and desserts. Because glucose is our cell's primary source of energy, it is the most important energy source. Carbohydrates are used for a variety of purposes aside from taste. Some are required to create the DNA found inside your cells. Certain carbohydrates, such as dietary fiber, aid in the health of your digestive system. Carbohydrates, like proteins, play an important structural role in the membranes that surround your body's cells. Whole grains, fruits, and vegetables are the best sources of carbohydrates. Man-made carbohydrates, such as pasta, should be considered secondary, and it is best to limit or avoid refined sugars.

Fat-

Fats can be found in oils, foods, and the human body. They provide energy to the body, are necessary for cell membrane structure, and are required for the development of your nervous and reproductive systems.

Just remember to eat more omega 3 fatty acids than omega 6 fatty acids.

Fatty fish, omega 3, flax seed oil, nuts, seeds, extra virgin olive oil, avocados, and cheese are the best sources of fat.

Water-

During bulking, it is critical to consume the appropriate amount of water. Water accounts for roughly 60% of your total body weight, so staying hydrated is critical. Its functions are critical because it aids in the transportation of nutrients, gases, and waste products. Water also aids in the regulation of your body temperature and the protection of your internal organs. The recommended daily water intake for adult females is 2.7 liters and men should drink at least 3.7 liters of water per day.

Vitamins

Vitamins can be found in almost any food, but they are widely present in fruits, vegetables, and grains. Vitamins are required by the body to regulate chemical reactions and promote growth and development. Some vitamins are known as antioxidants, and they help to protect your body from toxins such as air pollution. Water and fat-soluble vitamins are the two types of vitamins. A, D, E, and K are fat-soluble vitamins, while B and C are water-soluble vitamins. Raw fruits and vegetables, grains, meats, and dairy products are the best sources of vitamins.

Minerals-

The earth contains minerals such as iron, selenium, and sodium. Except for water, minerals are classified as inorganic substances. Most minerals are essential nutrients, each with its own function. As an example, sodium aids in the regulation of water balance in the body. Minerals are not used as an energy source, but they do aid in the production of energy. Because minerals are found in all foods, a balanced diet of carbohydrates, fats, and protein should result in no deficiencies and help you in proper bulking.

Train frequently with more volume

Train a muscle more frequently to increase training volume without doing too much in a single session which can lead to excessive soreness, low stimulus work sets, and injury. Training more frequently and in higher volumes is essential during a bulking phase. Because you have a caloric surplus and are well-fed, you can often train at a higher volume and still recover. It is critical to understand the training volume ranges that work best for you. This can be accomplished by training between 12 and 20 total weekly sets and monitoring recovery, soreness, and progression in the gym. In general, begin a program at the low end of the range and gradually increase the total volumes over the month. There is an upper limit to training volume, so keep track of your progress and recovery, and concentrate on effective work sets rather than endless volume.

Train a Wide Range of Rep Ranges

Most repetition ranges can be used to build muscle, according to research; however, when training frequently and in high volumes, repetition ranges work best to balance out the volume, training intensity, and recovery needs. For the majority of lifters, training movements in the 8-15 rep range will cover the majority of the bases for muscle growth. When performing compound exercises such as squats, bench presses, and deadlifts, it is best to train in the 5-10 rep range.

Train as close to muscle failure as possible

It is critical to train with intensity to push the muscles to near failure when training for muscle growth. I recommend pushing each set to near failure, leaving 1-2 perfect reps. Training to near muscle failure is not the same as training to complete failure. Make sure to push your sets hard, but never lose sight of technique. So, while performing the exercise, keep the main focus on maintaining proper posture.

Sleep enough

Sleep is essential for muscle healing and growth. As cliche as it may sound, obtaining at least 7-8 hours of sleep or more will help the nervous system, adrenals, and muscles recover faster. Additionally, obtaining adequate sleep helps enhance muscle growth and improve fat loss and metabolism by increasing hormone production, such as growth hormone.

Muscle gain during a bulk is an excellent way to improve long-term muscle growth and strength gain. When looking to bulk up quickly, it is also important to understand your body's rate of gain, as gaining too much weight too quickly can result in excessive body fat gain.

As we learned how to gain muscle quicker with the help of proper nutrition, training, and rest still, there is no way women can bulk up just because of heavy lifting. While weight lifting may appear intimidating at first, there is nothing to be concerned about. There are numerous advantages of lifting weights that you may miss out on if you are too fearful. Hopefully, these facts have eased your fear of "bulking up" and encouraged you to begin strength training for yourself.

FOUR

Myth -4- Weight lifting turns fat into muscles and your muscle will turn into fat if you stop working out

There is another big misconception is that Weight lifting turns fat into muscles and your muscle will turn into fat if you stop working out, many believe that if you keep doing strength training for a long time you will turn your fat into muscles and the fat comes back once you stop working out. Again, it is a myth that you can convert fat to muscle. Fat is taken from fat cells during weight loss and used to produce energy in the body, along with other by-products. Muscle is best preserved by strength training and eating a protein-rich diet. In this chapter, we are going to talk about these both tissues and how they are different from each other, their composition, their work and properties, and how they cannot transform into each other under any circumstances.

The difference between muscle and fat

Firstly, Let's try to understand the difference between Muscle and Fat. Muscle is classified into three types: skeletal, cardiac (heart), and smooth (mostly found in the intestine). Skeletal muscle, which is attached to bones by tendons and allows for voluntary movement of the body, is the most commonly thought of muscle in terms of body composition. The human body contains over 600 muscles. Some muscles assist you in moving, lifting, or sitting still. Others assist you in digesting food, breathing, and seeing. Your heart is a muscular organ that circulates blood throughout your body. Many injuries and diseases can affect how the muscles work. Maintain a healthy weight and exercise regularly to keep your muscles strong.

What are muscles?

Muscles are soft tissues. Your muscles are made up of many stretchy fibers. Different muscles perform different functions. Some muscles assist you in running, jumping, or performing delicate tasks such as threading a needle. Other muscles are responsible for breathing and digestion. Your heart is a busy muscle that beats thousands of times per day. A healthy lifestyle allows your muscles to function properly. Maintaining a healthy weight, eating a balanced diet, and getting plenty of exercise can help you keep your muscles strong.

Type of Muscles

You use your nervous system to control some muscles voluntarily. You make them move by thinking of yourself moving them. Other muscles work involuntarily, which means they are uncontrollable. They carry out their duties automatically. They function by taking cues from other body systems, such as your digestive or cardiovascular systems. The body contains three types of muscle tissue. They are as follows:

- Skeletal Muscle

These muscles, which are part of the musculoskeletal system, work collaboratively with your bones, tendons, and ligaments. Tendons connect skeletal muscles to bones throughout your body. They support your body's weight and allow you to move. You have control over these voluntary muscles. Some muscle fibers contract rapidly and require brief bursts of energy (fast-twitch muscles). Others move more slowly, such as your back muscles, which aid in posture. Skeletal muscles are made up of several different fibers. Fibers are made up of proteins called actin and myosin. The fiber bundles form a spindle shape (long and straight with tapered ends). Each spindle is surrounded by a membrane. Because of the striped pattern the spindles make together, providers characterize skeletal muscles as striated (striped).

- Cardiac Muscle

The heart's walls are lined by these muscles. They assist your heart in pumping blood via your cardiovascular system. You have no command over heart muscles. They contract when your heart instructs them to. These striated muscles resemble skeletal muscles in appearance. The fibers of heart muscles are made up of special cells called cardiomyocytes. Cardiomyocytes assist the heart in beating.

- Smooth Muscle

The insides of organs like the bladder, stomach, and intestines are lined with these muscles. Smooth muscles are involved in numerous physiological systems, including the female and male reproductive systems, the urinary system, and the respiratory system. These muscles function without you needing to think about it. They carry waste through your intestines and aid in the expansion of your lungs when you breathe. Smooth muscle fibers are made up of the proteins actin and myosin. These proteins come together in skeletal muscles to produce a spindle shape. These proteins are found in sheets in smooth muscles. The sheets make the muscle tissue appear smooth.

What happens to muscles during and after exercise?

Many people experience muscle soreness after exercising. When you apply stress on a muscle, microscopic rips (microtears) occur, causing pain. Muscle soreness usually appears a day or two after intensive exercise. This is why the condition is known as delayed onset muscle soreness (DOMS). Muscle tissue becomes inflamed as it repairs itself and the tiny tears heal. Your muscles will recover and the inflammation will lessen within a few days. Muscle tissue tears and rebuilds repeatedly as a result of continued exercise. Muscles grow in size as a result of this process.

What is Fat?

Fats are also known as 'fatty acids' or 'lipids.' Our body's fats are made up of three molecules linked together. A "triglyceride" is a three-molecule structure. Our bodies produce the majority of the fat we require, but there are some fats that our bodies cannot produce. These fats can only be obtained by eating them. These fats are referred to as "essential" fats because we must obtain them from food. Omega-3 fats (found in foods such as fish and flaxseed) and Omega-6 fats are examples of essential fats (found in foods such as nuts, seeds, and corn oil)

Type of body fat and their functions

- White

The most common type of fat is white fat. It is composed of large, white cells that are stored beneath the skin or around organs in the abdomen, arms, buttocks, and thighs. These fat cells serve as the body's energy storage system. This type of fat is also important in the function of hormones such as estrogen, leptin (a hunger hormone), insulin, cortisol (a stress hormone), and growth hormone. While some white fat is beneficial to health, too much white fat is extremely harmful. The percentage of healthy body fat varies according to your level of fitness or physical activity. According to the American Council on Exercise, men should have a total body fat percentage of 14 to 24 percent, while women should have a total body fat percentage of 21 to 31 percent. A higher than recommended body fat percentage can put you at risk for the following health problems: Diabetes type 2, coronary artery disease, hypertension, stroke, hormone imbalances, pregnancy complications, kidney disease, liver disease, and cancer.

- Brown

Brown fat is primarily found in babies, though adults do retain a small amount of brown fat, usually in the neck and shoulders. To keep you warm, this type of fat burns fatty acids. Researchers are looking for ways to stimulate brown fat activity in order to help prevent obesity.

- Beige (brite)

Beige (or brite) fat research is still in its early stages. These fat cells are intermediate in function between brown and white fat cells. Beige cells, like brown fat, can help burn fat rather than store it. Certain hormones and enzymes that are released when you are stressed, cold, or exercising are thought to help convert white fat to beige fat. This is an exciting area of research that could aid in the prevention of obesity and the maintenance of healthy body fat levels.

- Essential Fat

Essential fat is exactly what it sounds like: it's necessary for your life and a healthy body. This fat can be found in your brain, bone marrow, nerves, and organ membranes. Essential fat regulates hormones, including those that control fertility, vitamin absorption, and temperature regulation. To be in good health, women need at least 10 to 13 percent of their body composition to come from essential fat, while men need at least 2 to 5 percent.

- Subcutaneous fat

Subcutaneous fat is fat that is stored beneath the skin. It is made up of brown, beige, and white fat cells. Subcutaneous fat accounts for the vast majority of our body fat. It's the fat on your arms, belly, thighs, and buttocks that you can squeeze or pinch. Calipers are used by fitness professionals to measure subcutaneous fat to estimate total body fat percentage. A certain amount of subcutaneous fat is normal and healthy, but too much can cause hormonal imbalances and sensitivity.

- Visceral fat

Visceral fat, also known as "belly fat," is the white fat found in your abdomen and surrounding all of your major organs, including the liver, kidneys, pancreas, intestines, and heart. High levels of visceral fat can put you at risk for diabetes, heart disease, stroke, artery disease, and some cancers.

Benefits of appropriate fat

Body composition is critical. With an appropriate overall fat percentage, your body will function optimally. A healthy body fat percentage has numerous advantages, including temperature regulation, balanced hormone levels, improved reproductive health, adequate vitamin storage, good neurological function, healthy metabolism, and balanced blood sugar.

Risk of having a high-fat percentage

Too much white fat, especially visceral fat, can be detrimental to your health. Visceral fat can put you at risk for the following health problems: heart disease, stroke, coronary artery disease, atherosclerosis, pregnancy complications, type 2 diabetes, hormone disturbances, some cancers

Body fat percentage

Several methods exist for measuring body composition. Skinfold measurements are a common method for estimating body fat percentage. Calipers, a tong-like instrument, can be used by a trained technician to pinch and measure skin folds on your arms, waist, and thighs to estimate total body fat percentage. This method primarily measures subcutaneous fat.

Another option is to use a device known as the Bod Pod. During a body composition analysis, the device calculates total fat percentage based on body weight and volume ratios. This method, in theory, measures all types of fat in your body.

Another method for calculating body fat percentage is bioelectrical impedance analysis. It's commonly found in athletic training facilities. This test involves standing on a device that measures the amount of lean versus fatty mass in your body using an electrical current.

BMI and waist circumference measurements may also be useful. They don't give you a specific percentage of body fat, but they do give you an estimate based on your height and weight. BMI is calculated as a weight-to-height ratio, whereas waist circumference is a measurement of the narrowest part of the waist.

A BMI greater than 25 is considered overweight, while a BMI greater than 30 is considered obese, according to the National Institutes of Health (NIH). A waist circumference of more than 35 inches in women and 40 inches in men is associated with an increased risk of disease, as increased waist circumference can indicate the presence of visceral fat.

The most important takeaway from the preceding information is that there are three types of fat cells in the body: white, brown, and beige. Fat cells can be stored in three different ways: essential fat, subcutaneous fat, and visceral fat. A healthy, functional body requires essential fat. Subcutaneous fat is found beneath the skin and accounts for the majority of our body fat. This is how the body stores energy for later use.

Functions of Lipids in the Body

Fats in the body are essential for energy storage, body temperature regulation, cushioning vital organs, hormone regulation, nerve impulse transmission, and transporting fat-soluble nutrients. Fats in food provide a concentrated energy source, improve food texture and flavor, and promote satiety. Excess energy from food is stored in the body as adipose tissue.

Fat is Energy Storage

Excess energy from food is digested and incorporated into adipose tissue, also known as fat tissue. Carbohydrates and lipids provide the majority of the energy required by the human body; in fact, fat accounts for 30-70 percent of the energy used during rest. As previously stated, glucose is stored in the body as glycogen. While glycogen is a ready source of energy, lipids serve primarily as an energy reserve. Glycogen is quite bulky and has high water content, so the body cannot store an excessive amount for an extended period of time. During exercise, fat is used for energy, especially after glycogen is depleted. Without water, fats pack together tightly and store far more energy in a smaller space. A fat gram is densely concentrated with energy, containing more than twice as much as a carbohydrate gram. Unlike other body cells that can only store a limited amount of fat, fat cells are specialized for fat storage and can expand almost permanently in size.

In conclusion, no matter how hard you try, you can't turn fat into muscle. Muscle cannot be converted into fat. Fat and muscle are two distinct types of tissue that cannot be converted into each other. Fat is made up of triglycerides. Each of these tiny fatty molecules is shaped like a capital E, with three fatty acid chains made of carbon, hydrogen, and oxygen. The building blocks of muscle are nitrogen-containing amino acid chains. Fat cannot transform into muscle because it lacks nitrogen. But fat loss and muscle building are possible simultaneously with a different processes.Combining a diet plan in deficit calories with moderate-intensity cardio such as walking or cycling with strength training such as lifting weights or resistance band exercises is the greatest way to burn fat and build muscle.

FIVE

MYTH -5- CARDIO IS BETTER THAN WEIGHT TRAINING FOR FAT LOSS

Cardio is better than weight training for losing fat is a very common belief, but in this chapter, we are going to look into science-based facts that claim otherwise. In fact, on this subject, the research is very clear that weight lifting is undoubtedly superior to cardiovascular training for a variety of reasons. Before we go deep to understand if cardio is better or weight training for fat loss, we need to understand the difference between weight loss and fat loss. Weight loss is defined as a decrease in overall body weight caused by muscle, water, and fat loss. Fat loss is weight loss from fat, which is a more specific and healthy goal than weight loss. Many weight loss programs claim that they can help you to lose weight quickly and easily. However, it is important to note that a significant portion of this weight may be due to water and muscle loss and muscle loss can be harmful because it is an important component of overall health. Maintaining a healthy muscle percentage has several benefits, including regulating healthy blood sugar levels, maintaining healthy fat levels in the blood (such as triglycerides and cholesterol), and controlling inflammation.

For a clearer understanding of fat loss through cardio and weight training firstly, we need to understand the benefits of both training, here are some important benefits of doing cardio and weight training are followings.

benefits of cardio

1. Improves heart health

Aerobic exercise improves circulation, lowering blood pressure and heart rate. Furthermore, it improves your overall aerobic fitness, as well as your cardiac output (how well your heart pumps). Aerobic exercise also lowers the risk of developing type 2 diabetes and, if you already have diabetes, helps you control your blood glucose levels. Ideally, at least 30 minutes a day, five days a week of cardio is considered effective, which can be included walking, running, swimming, cycling, playing tennis and jumping rope, etc.

1. Regulates appetite

According to one study, people who did high-intensity cardio ate 11% less in the 24 hours afterward. Exercising at such a high level causes your body to circulate more blood to avoid overheating. As a result, blood is diverted away from your stomach and around your body, putting the brakes on your appetite.

3. Aids fat loss

Because of the continuous nature of intensity, cardiovascular exercise burns more calories per minute than weight training. As a result, doing cardio for weight loss can assist you in losing body fat.

However, depending on your goal, the type of cardio you choose is important:

LISS (low-intensity steady-state cardio) is ideal for those with large weight loss goals, is suitable for beginners, and can aid in the reduction of stubborn body fat.

HIIT (high-intensity interval training) is ideal for retaining existing muscle, stimulating fat-burning enzymes, and efficiently burning fat.

4. Boosts brain power

Our brains gradually lose tissue as we age. This process begins around the age of 30 and has a significant impact on our cognitive performance. Cardiovascular exercise has been linked to a significant reduction in the amount of brain tissue lost over time, with one study finding that those who exercised in this manner regularly had the most 'strong' brain tissue.

5. Maintain blood pressure levels

If you have high blood pressure, cardiovascular exercise can help you lower it to healthy levels. One study found that steady-state cardio: walking, jogging, cycling, and swimming was effective in lowering blood pressure levels in moderately active adults.

6. Improves immune system

A strong immune system has always been important, and fortunately, getting some daily cardio movement in will help keep your immune system running at peak efficiency. According to research, "regular and moderate exercise has beneficial effects on the immune system by increasing "immunoglobulins," which are immune-system protecting molecules produced by your white blood cells.

Benefits of weight training

1. Builds muscle

We all know that lifting weights can help you build and tone your muscles. Weight training puts more strain on your muscles, causing the tissue to break down faster. This activates the body's response to clean up and heal the tissue, resulting in muscle growth as well as increased strength and endurance. The technical term for this is 'hypertrophy.'

2. Boosts metabolism and fat loss

Weight training helps you in losing body fat. To put it simply, weight training equals increased lean muscle mass, which equals a higher metabolic rate, which equals more calories burned.

While cardiovascular exercise will most likely burn more calories, weight training will keep that slow burn going all day, resulting in a larger and more sustained calorie burn over the day. Because muscle is more metabolically active than fat, the more muscle you gain, the more calories you'll burn, and the more likely you are to lose fat.

3. Protects bones and increases bone health

Weight-bearing exercises, whether bodyweight or with added resistance, aid in bone health. Weight-bearing exercises that promote bone health include walking, jogging, lunging, squatting, and light circuits. The key is to not overdo it; excessive exercise can be harmful to joints. Three times per week for at least half an hour is sufficient.

4. Relieves stress

Lifting a weight that was previously beyond your ability or comfort zone can make you feel strong and put your daily stress on the back foot.

5. Aids sleep

Weight training relieves stress and aids in sleep. Weight training, according to Clinics in Sports Medicine, tires your muscles while the drop in cortisol allows you to sleep more peacefully all night.

So, which is better for fat loss: cardio or weights?

Muscles are similar to small-calorie factors. The more muscle you have or the more active it is, the more calories you burn even when you are not moving or while sleeping, watching TV, sitting at your desk at work, or reading this book. And those extra calories burned to add up. Furthermore, our bodies use calories to recover after a workout, and weight training requires more recovery than cardio. That is, after the workout, you typically burn more calories from weight lifting than you do from cardio. For example, suppose you burn 100 calories jogging and another 100 recovering afterward, for a total of 200 calories burned. Now assume you burn 150 calories lifting weights and another 300 recovering. That's a total of 450 calories, which is more than cardio training, even though the weight workout used fewer calories than jogging. The more you jog, the more efficient you become as a runner, and the fewer calories you burn to run the same distance. Weightlifting, on the other hand, is the total opposite. More calories are required for heavier lifts. It takes more energy to deadlift 500 pounds than it does to deadlift 100 pounds. As a result, as you get stronger, you throw more weight around and burn more calories. Aditionally, heavier lifts require more recovery time, which means more calories burned. Despite this, there is something to be said for cardio exercise. Cardiovascular exercise has been shown to specifically reduce visceral fat or belly fat. While it is obvious that weight training burns more fat than cardio, cardio training may target the waistline more specifically than weight lifting. This is a huge benefit, as many people are actively trying to lose weight around their midsection.

Weight training is more effective for fat loss and muscle building. Cardio, on the other hand, will aid in weight loss, cardiovascular health, and revealing the muscle you've sculpted. If you want to tone up while also sculpting muscle, mixing it up each week is the best way to achieve your body composition and aesthetic goals. It's a sort of union of both.

Both cardio and weight training are popular workouts, but deciding which is the better use of your time can be difficult.

Based on research, you can use your body weight to estimate how many calories you will burn during various types of exercise, such as cardio and weight training. For most activities, the more weight you have, the more calories you will burn. If you weigh 160 pounds (73 kg), jogging at a moderate pace for 30 minutes will burn about 250 calories. If you run at a faster pace of 6 miles per hour for 30 minutes, you would burn approximately 365 calories.

However, if you are weight trained for the same amount of time, you might only burn 130–220 calories.

In general, cardio will burn more calories per session than weight training for the same amount of effort. The number of calories burned during exercise is determined by your body size and the intensity with which you exercise. A cardio workout typically burns more calories than a weight training workout of the same duration. Although a weight-training workout does not typically burn as many calories as a cardio workout, it does have other significant advantages.

Weight training, for example, is more effective than cardio in terms of building muscle, and muscle burns more calories at rest than other tissues, such as fat. As a result, it is generally believed that muscle building is the key to increasing your resting metabolism, that is, how many calories you burn at rest.

One study measured participants' resting metabolisms during 24 weeks of weight training. Weight training resulted in a 9% increase in resting metabolism in men. The effects on women were smaller, with an increase of nearly 4%. While this may sound appealing, consider how many calories this represents. Resting metabolism increased by about 140 calories per day in men. It was only about 50 calories per day for women. Thus, weight training and gaining a little muscle will not increase your metabolism dramatically, but it may increase it slightly.

However, weight training has additional calorie-burning benefits. Specifically, research has shown that a weight training session burns more calories in the hours later than a cardio workout. In fact, resting metabolism has been reported to remain elevated for up to 38 hours after weight training, whereas no such increase has been reported with cardio. This means that the calorie-burning benefits of weight do not stop when you exercise. You may continue to burn calories for hours or days afterward. A more intense workout will increase the number of calories you burn afterward for most types of weight training exercises.

HIIT for Fat Loss

Although cardio and weight training are two of the most popular exercises, there are some others too. High-intensity interval training (HIIT) is one of these, and it consists of short bursts of very intense exercise followed by low-intensity recovery periods. A HIIT workout typically lasts 10–30 minutes. HIIT can be combined with a variety of exercises, including sprinting, biking, jump roping, and other body-weight exercises. Some studies have compared the effects of cardio, weight training, and HIIT. In one study, the calories burned during 30 minutes of HIIT, weight training, running, and biking were compared. The researchers discovered that HIIT burned 25–30% more calories than the other types of exercise. This is not to say that other types of exercise aren't beneficial for weight loss. Other studies have found that HIIT-style workouts may burn roughly the same number of calories as traditional cardio, though this depends on the intensity of the exercise. According to some research, if you weigh about 160 pounds (73 kg), you can burn about 300 calories in 30 minutes of either cardio or HIIT. One of the potential benefits of HIIT is that you can spend less time actually exercising because rest periods are included between the intense periods of activity. High-intensity interval training (HIIT) can help you burn calories quickly. According to some studies, it may burn more calories than weights or cardio. Overall, it can produce similar weight loss comparable to cardio, but with less time spent exercising.

In conclusion, cardio burns more calories than weight training when both are done for the same amount of time, but weight training is more effective at decreasing body fat. Weight training is also better than cardio for building muscle. Furthermore, the more muscle mass you have, the more calories you burn at rest. This is the primary reason why men have higher calorie requirements than women. As a result, losing muscle weight can reduce the number of calories you burn at rest, making it easier to regain any fat weight you lost. There are a few simple ways to ensure that you lose fat while maintaining or gaining muscle mass. These include eating plenty of protein, exercising regularly, and sticking to a nutrient-dense diet with a slight calorie deficit. The greatest mix is to do cardio and weight training on different days. Do full-body lifts every time you lift on weight-training days, meaning every muscle group in your body. That's how you'll get the most out of it and burn the most calories. The most crucial aspects of weight loss are nutrition and sleep, but a mix of three days of weight training and two days of cardio training can offer you the finest fat loss results.

SIX

MYTH -6- WOMEN SHOULD NOT DO EXERCISE DURING THE MENSTRUATION CYCLE

One common myth that people believe is that women should not exercise during their menstrual cycle. This myth, like many others, is entirely baseless. Many myths surround the menstrual cycle, but this is the most common. For some, it is a genuine belief instilled by years of being told by parents and grandparents. Others use it as an excuse to avoid exercising. Women are told not to exercise during their periods by their coaches, fitness experts, family elders, and female peers. The reasons given range from increasing discomfort to "poor health" to injury risk. Some athletes compete and win while on their period. They cannot change their competition dates, and they do not train any less in the lead-up to the competition. This scenario may seem harsh, but it applies to all women. Rather than suggesting it's okay to exercise during the period, let's say that it's beneficial to do so.

Studies have shown that women who exercise consistently have more comfortable periods throughout their cycles. It balances the hormone system so that cycles are less painful, bloating is reduced, and the flow is not excessive. Water is flushed from the body when they sweat, reducing abdominal bloating. Exercise also generates mood-enhancing endorphins, which make them less aware of discomfort in general. According to a recent study, better levels of exercise are linked to reduced PMS symptoms. It could potentially be a good time to exercise. Because estrogen and progesterone levels drop during the period, they may easily access carbohydrate/glycogen, resulting in a faster fat breakdown.

Having said that, women must be aware of their bodies and learn to recognize signs. Slow down but don't stop if working out at the usual pace leaves them exhausted. Other women may experience more abdominal discomfort as a result of certain exercises. In this case, modify exercises or temporarily discontinue them while continuing to work out. Taking a day or two off is also perfectly acceptable. What is not acceptable is to believe that you must NOT exercise during the period.

Let's get a little deeper into it and try to understand the whole physiology behind it and how a woman can work, cook and compete while she is on her periods.

Hormones are messengers in your body, coursing through your veins carrying orders from your organs to your brain and from brain to organs to perform nearly everything you do. Hormones instruct your body on when to eat, sleep, and even grow. They satisfy our hunger and other needs. They are in charge of having children. They make us feel happy, sad, and in love. These hormones are fairly consistent in men day in and day out. Women, on the other hand, are a different story. And the story revolves around the menstrual cycle. The menstrual cycle not only affects fertility and moods but can also have a significant impact on training and performance. Despite this, very few coaches and trainers, even in the most elite competitive sectors, consider it with their athletes. Many people, coaches, trainers, and even doctors are ashamed of talking about periods publicly, Until recently, female athletes were hesitant to discuss their "periods" on a public platform. Although things have improved, there is still a long way to go. After winning the bronze medal in 2016, Chinese swimmer Fu Yuanhui admitted to having her period during the 2016 Summer Olympics. She had also clarified that she was not using her period as an excuse. Looking into sports like tennis where female athletes have to complete almost every week and they don't have a choice to skip the competition or in that case even the training. So the only option left is to train and compete and get used to it, as a man I might not able to feel the pain and suffering behind the mensuration but we have seen examples have been set before by women where women broke records, set another milestone and competed fiercely during their periods and if they can achieve it, others can too. In this chapter, I am going to talk more about athletes but it does not mean that an ordinary office-going or housemaker cannot take learning from it, it is going to be an obvious understanding that if a female can compete, jump, run, play highest level of competition it means any woman with any kind of profession will be able to manage her work efficiently during her periods.

Every month, women experience two hormone phases: high and low. Women's carbohydrate metabolism and recovery during the low-hormone phase are physiologically similar to men's. But It's a different story when women's hormones rise during the other half of the month. High estrogen levels cause them to preserve glycogen and increase the amount of fat we use as fuel. High progesterone slows women's sweat response, raises core temperature, increases sodium loss, and increases muscle breakdown, while also restricting their ability to synthesize muscle because they can't access the protein building blocks, amino acids. After ovulation, a woman's hormones rapidly increase leading to their period, the one-two punch of high estrogen and progesterone causes fluids to shift into the cells (bloat), lowers blood plasma volume, and makes them more inclined to central nervous system fatigue, making exercise feel harder than usual. All of this is especially annoying when they've been training for months, maybe years, and their competition clashes with their period when hormones are at their peak. Women must work with it instead of against their natural physiology to succeed. Menstruation is a small point when it comes to the physiological differences between males and females, and it's time for women to have the fitness and nutrition knowledge they need to compete on an equal playing field with men. Women not only require different fuels before and during exercise, but they also have different recovery requirements. Their recovery window is much shorter than men's; it's more difficult to retain valuable muscle tissue, and they are more vulnerable to performance issues in the heat.

Women are smaller and lighter than men, and they have a higher percentage of body fat. But as you dig deeper, the comparisons become more interesting and revealing. Let's start with body mass and how it's distributed. Mass is the stuff we're made of, which everyone commonly refers to as the weight of the number on the scale, which is not entirely correct. Weight is technically determined by gravitational pull, so you would weigh far less on the moon and far more on Earth. The number you see on the scale is your weight, which fluctuates widely depending on fluid intake, what you've eaten during the day, salt intake, and how much glycogen you're storing in your muscles. Body mass, on the other hand, is the actual stuff you're made of—bone, muscle, fat, and organs—which requires tissue loss or gain and is more difficult to change.

According to research, men's and women's shoulder, biceps, and quadriceps muscle fibers are very similar. Men and women have similar muscle compositions in terms of the percentage of type I endurance (aerobic) and type I power (anaerobic) fibers. What differentiates women's bodies is that the largest fibers are type I endurance fibers, whereas men's bodies are dominated by type I power fibers. It means that when it comes to strength comparisons, women fall a little short. According to studies, women are about 52% as strong as men in their upper bodies and 66% as strong in their lower bodies. These strength differences subside slightly in well-muscled women. When measured in terms of overall strength relative to lean body mass, a trained woman's strength in the arms and legs is 70 and 80 percent that of men, respectively. Still less powerful, but much closer. Women may outperform men in the leg press because they tend to carry the majority of our lean muscle tissue below the waist. And now let's look at the fat distribution between men and women. Women and men store fat in different ways. While fat distribution varies from person to person and is mostly determined by genetic factors, women are more likely to be pear-shaped than men. Women tend to store fat in their buttocks, hips, lower abdomen, and thighs. A woman's thighs store the fat she needs for pregnancy and nursing. Women's bodies are built to hold more fat than men's. An active woman will have 21 percent to 24 percent body fat, while a guy will have 14 percent to 17 percent, according to the American Council on Exercise. To function correctly, both men and women must maintain a particular level of necessary fat. For example, women should have no less than 10% body fat, whereas men just need 2%. This is because a mother's body must be capable of caring for a growing infant, and fat stores assist her in doing so. Estrogen production during puberty allows women to generate these required fat reserves.

So the question is, can women do exercise during the mensuration cycle? The answer is Yes. Everyone worries about having their period and continuing with exercise or sport, but in reality, their hormones are favorable for performance once their period starts. As we already know that women experience two hormone phases: high and low. As strange as it may seem, women's exercise physiology during their period and the days that follow is almost identical to that of a man. Women are also stronger at that time. According to research, when women strength train during their low-hormone phase, they gain more strength and produce more force than when they train during their high-hormone phase. They also experience less pain and recover faster. When they're in the low-hormone phase of the cycle, which begins on the first day of menstrual flow, it will feel easier to work out, train, or compete. During the premenstrual stage of the cycle, women should consume extra carbohydrates, especially if they're exercising for long periods. In general, aim for a combination of 10 to 15 grams of protein and 40 grams of carbohydrates (approximately 200 to 220 calories) before any workout longer than 90 minutes, then 40 to 50 grams of carbohydrates every hour when working out.

It is important to note that women burn more calories overall during the premenstrual period. According to studies, there is a 5 to 10% increase in metabolism in the days before they start bleeding. This equates to an additional 100 to 200 calories. This is the reason for cravings for chocolates and chips. They could be bloated because high estrogen and progesterone affect the hormones that regulate fluid in the body.

Exercises To Do During Periods

There are many myths about exercising during this period, but exercise has been shown to help with a variety of symptoms associated with the cycle. Symptoms like Abdominal cramps, Stomach upset diarrhea, nausea, vomiting, Headache, Bloating, Mood swings, irritability, and fatigue are common during periods. According to research, these symptoms are caused by a variety of physical and hormonal changes in the female body. Proper exercise can help to balance these physical and hormonal changes by increasing the production of endorphins (feel-good hormones) and decreasing irritability and pain, thereby improving their mood. Some of the benefits of exercising during periods include decreased PMS symptoms, experiencing an endorphin release, gaining more strength and power, fighting period pains, and also mood can be better too. Due to abdominal cramps and heavy bleeding, the first few days of a period can be difficult. Exercise can be a savior during these difficult times. Athletes should continue with their normal daily routine, and for non-athletes here are a few simple workouts to keep them healthy and happy.

Walking –

During periods, the best exercise is a simple, light walk. This low-intensity aerobic exercise improves the function of the lungs later in the cycle. These will also help to improve mood and burn some calories. These light movements of the body increase endorphin secretion as well.

Yoga-

Many yoga poses help to improve blood circulation and relieve noxious complaints. Yoga has been scientifically proven to help relax the female body and relieve period symptoms such as cramps and bloating.

Running-

Running can instantly reduce pain and irritability. Go for a slow run, taking short breaks in between if necessary.

Light weight lifting-

Light weight lifting at home or in the gym can improve muscle flexibility and strength.

Swimming-

Swimming is one of the most relaxing and gentle exercises that can be done when on period. Females bleed less when swimming in cold water because the cold tightens blood vessels for a short period.

Dancing-

Dancing is a fun activity that can improve the mood while also burning calories. Zumba is another entertaining and creative option.

Pilates-

Pilates is currently the most popular type of workout. It aids in the relaxation of the female body and the maintenance of health and well-being. Pilates targets specific muscle groups, allowing the workout to be personalized to the individual's needs. Pilates strengthens the core, which can lessen the severity of cramps.

Stretching-

Simple stretches at home can also be beneficial; if other exercises cause discomfort, try stretching and taking deep breaths to relax the muscles.

Exercising during periods can be a lot beneficial but certain things should be avoided during periods –

- Rigorous activities should be avoided.
- Avoid doing exercises for a long period.
- Yoga inversion poses are not advised.

For example, Downward-Facing Dog (Adho Mukha Svanasana), Legs up the Wall (Viparita Karani), Child's Pose (Balasana), Forward Fold Pose

- listen to the body and know when to stop

While exercise can provide the previously stated benefits, going too far can have an equally negative impact. Excessive exercise can cause women to miss their periods entirely. If this occurs, it is best to reduce the intensive exercise routine. A regular menstrual cycle is a sign of good health.

Food to eat during the period

It's difficult to predict how they will feel during their period. While some women have no symptoms, others have difficulty getting out of bed due to cramping, headaches, pain, and nausea. But here are some healthy food options to help them feel better.

Dark Chocolate-

It is without a doubt one of the most popular foods to eat during the period for a variety of reasons. Dark chocolate, which is high in antioxidants and magnesium, is an excellent source for providing comfort.

Oatmeal-

Oatmeal is a whole grain that is high in calcium, vitamins A and B, and iron. One study found that eating more of the type of iron found in oatmeal was associated with a lower risk of PMS symptoms. Oatmeal is also a good option if you have an upset stomach.

Salmon

This fish is high in omega-3 fatty acids and is known for its antioxidant and anti-inflammatory properties, which help to relax the uterus and fight cramps. Consider preparing grilled salmon as a meal for a boost of high-quality protein and B vitamins.

Watermelons, plums, and figs-

The natural sugars in these foods may satisfy sweet cravings. Besides this, these fruits are high in vitamins, which can help with bloating. Watermelon is high in water and can help keep your body hydrated, reducing swelling and bloating.

Citrus

Oranges, lemons, and limes are a healthy alternative to sugary treats because they are high in fiber and vitamin C and can help with mood swings and bloating. Their high water content helps in hydration as well.

Eggs

Egg yolks are high in iron, fat-soluble minerals, B vitamins, vital fatty acids, and protein, all of which help with PMS.

Tea-

Tea could be a good option for over-the-counter pain relievers for menstrual cramps. While various teas may help relieve period cramping and pain, ginger tea, green tea, thyme tea, and oolong tea are the ones with scientific data to back them up.

Food to avoid during the period

During menstruation, women lose blood while also experiencing significant hormonal changes. Choose foods high in vitamins, minerals, water, protein, iron, and fiber. Simultaneously, do your best to prevent the following.

Processed Food-

Bloating and water retention can be increased by canned foods, overly processed meat, and other foods containing chemicals and additives. High sodium levels are bad at any time of the month, but they're especially bad during the period.

Spicy foods-

Spicy foods should be avoided during the menstrual cycle because the gut is already on fire. Spicy foods can worsen stomach health, resulting in ulcers and increased abdominal pain.

Candy and snacks-

To satisfy sweet cravings, choose juicy fruit instead of sweet snacks. as they cause bloating and gas while providing a short-term blood sugar spike.

Alcohol and Smoking-

Reduce or eliminate the drinking of alcohol while on period. Because the loss of blood at this time lowers blood pressure and women are more vulnerable to the side effects of alcohol during this time. It also worsens fatigue and increases menstrual flow. According to the ACOG, women who smoke have more severe premenstrual symptoms and a 50% increase in cramps that last two or more days.

In Conclusion, during their periods, women may have symptoms such as stomach upset, bloating, exhaustion, cramps, and headache. Physical activity may aid in the reduction of these and other symptoms. Other health benefits of exercise include a better mood, fewer menstrual cramps, and less exhaustion. Women may need to modify their regular exercise program while on their period and also need to understand that staying active is much more beneficial than staying in bed.

SEVEN

Myth -7- People with Asthma or any other respiratory issues should not be the part of sports or do any physical activities

There are myths around the Indian community that people with Asthma or any other respiratory issues should not be part of sports or should not do much physical activity. There are many breathing and lungs related diseases found in India but Asthma is most commonly known by people. In this chapter, we are going to understand Asthma in deep and know playing a sport or doing any kind of physical activity is completely fine with a little bit of care. Among India's 1.31 billion people, about 6% of children and 2% of adults have asthma. Asthma is widely stigmatized in India, and many people hide the condition. Asthma mortality in India decreased from 1990 to 2005, especially in richer states and metropolitan regions with better healthcare facilities. Uttar Pradesh and Rajasthan have the highest death rates in India, which are being addressed by health officials. Let's try to understand asthma in detail.

Asthmatic people and their families frequently see asthma as a barrier to physical activity. Asthma, a common but serious chronic disease, affects about one out of every ten children. Asthma that is not well controlled can cause devasting symptoms, school absences, and life-threatening events that demand emergency treatment. Asthma can interrupt a one's ability to play, learn, and sleep, all of which are important for his or her development. People with asthma should be able to participate fully in all activities, including vigorous exercise if their asthma is well managed and controlled. As a teacher, physical education teacher, coach, or trainer who supervises the person participating in physical activity, you can use practical strategies to reduce the burden of asthma on that individual and family.

What is Asthma?

Asthma is a severe chronic lung disease that causes inflammation and narrowing of the airways. Although inflammation is a beneficial defense mechanism for our bodies, it can be harmful if it occurs at the wrong time or persists after it is no longer required. When a person has asthma, this is what happens. Ongoing inflammation (swelling) makes the airways in the lungs more sensitive to things they perceive as foreign and harmful, such as bacteria, viruses, dust, tobacco smoke, and strong odors, which are also referred to as asthma "triggers." The immune system of an asthmatic person overreacts to these stimuli by releasing various types of cells and chemicals that cause changes in the airways. Like, the inner linings of the airways become inflamed (swollen), making less room for air to pass through. The muscles surrounding the airways tighten, further narrowing the airways. The mucus glands in the airways produce a lot of thick mucus, which blocks the airways even more. Asthmatics may find it more difficult to breathe as a result of these changes. They can also cause coughing, wheezing, chest tightness, and shortness of breath. If the inflammation associated with asthma is not treated, the inflammation increases each time the airways are exposed to their asthma triggers, and the person with asthma is more likely to have symptoms.

Exercise-Induced Asthma

Asthma that is triggered by physical activity is known as exercise-induced asthma. If a person's asthma is not well-controlled, vigorous exercise will trigger symptoms. Some people only have asthma symptoms when they exercise. Asthma symptoms differ from person to person and frequently from season to season or even hour to hour. Programs for asthmatic people may need to be temporarily modified at times, such as by varying the type, intensity, duration, and/or frequency of activity. People with asthma should be included in activities as much as possible at all times. Asthma is a chronic and dangerous disease, but the good news is that modern time asthma treatments are effective enough that most people can fully participate in regular activities, such as play, sports, and other physical activities.

Medications for Asthma

Many asthmatics require both long-term control and quick-relief medications. These medications both treat and prevent symptoms, allowing the person to participate in physical activities safely and fully. The majority of asthma medications are inhaled as sprays or powders and can be taken via metered-dose inhalers, dry powder inhalers, or nebulizers. A metered-dose inhaler is a pressurized canister that delivers medication without requiring deep and rapid breathing. Another type of inhaler is a dry powder inhaler, which requires deep and rapid breathing to get the medication into the lungs. A nebulizer is a machine that creates a fine mist from liquid medication. Whatever method of administration is used, everyone who has asthma must take their medications correctly. Long-term control medications are typically taken daily to control underlying airway inflammation and, as a result, to prevent asthma symptoms. Inhaled corticosteroids are the most effective long-term asthma control medications. It is important to remember that when used as directed, inhaled corticosteroids are generally safe for long-term use. They are not addictive and are not the same as the illegal anabolic steroids that some athletes use for performance enhancement. Quick-relief medications (also known as short-acting bronchodilators) are used to relieve asthma symptoms quickly and temporarily. They aid in the prevention of asthma attacks by temporarily relaxing the muscles surrounding the airways. They do not, however, address the underlying airway inflammation that is causing the symptoms to worsen. Quick-relief medications can also be used to prevent asthma symptoms in youth who have exercise-induced asthma. Health care providers may instruct them to use their quick-relief medication inhaler 5 minutes before engaging in physical activities and the coach and trainer should make sure that they do follow the given instruction by the doctors. Coaches, trainers, or anyone observing physical activities should ensure that a person with asthma has quick and easy access to their quick-relief medication. These people frequently require medication to treat asthma symptoms during school, office, college, workplace, or competition, or to take just before participating in physical activities or being exposed to another asthma trigger. If getting to the medication is difficult, inconvenient, or embarrassing, the person may become discouraged and fail to use his or her quick-relief as needed. Asthma in the individual may worsen unnecessarily, limiting his or her activities.

Exercising with Asthma

Team sports with short bursts of exertion, such as volleyball, gymnastics, baseball, and wrestling, are beneficial, as are solos or group leisure activities such as walking, biking, and hiking. Swimming is also a good option because it allows you to breathe in a lot of warm, moist air. It's also a great way to strengthen your upper body. Long periods of exertion, such as soccer, distance running, basketball, and field hockey, may be more difficult. Cold-weather sports, such as ice hockey, cross-country skiing, and ice skating, may also present difficulties. However, many people with asthma can fully participate in these activities. Aerobic exercise may cause an asthma attack in some people. They respond by avoiding physical activity. As a result, their fitness declines, and symptoms may appear with even light physical activity. However, exercise can help reduce the frequency and severity of these asthma attacks. As you become more active, you can learn how to control your asthma with proper treatment and precautions. Most people with asthma should be able to exercise with minimal problems or restrictions if they take the right medication. Obesity appears to increase the risk of asthma, according to growing evidence. If you are overweight, becoming more active will help you lose weight while also benefiting your asthma. The key is to select activities you enjoy. Making exercise a regular part of your routine can also have a significant positive impact on your overall health.

As we are clear that people with Asthma can do sports and also can take part in any kind of physical activity. Then questions arise that what kind of physical activity or sport is the better choice for asthmatic people. High-intensity exercise, in general, will cause more problems than longer durations. Furthermore, cold, dry air is more ready to trigger off an attack than warm, moist air. You will gradually become less breathless during the same amount of exercise as you gain fitness. Exercise also appears to reduce airway swelling and the severity and frequency of symptoms. The greatest health benefit occurs when inactive people become moderately active. Aim for 150 minutes of fast walking per week. Making exercise a habit can have a significant impact on your health. Begin with aerobic activity. Add resistance workouts gradually. Asthmatics on long-term oral corticosteroid treatment may experience muscle loss. This results in decreased strength, particularly in the lower limbs. If this is the case, you should probably start with strength training.

This will provide even more benefits to your overall health and well-being.

Important points to remember when exercising

- Consult your doctor before beginning an exercise program. They will assist you in determining which activities are best for you. They will devise an action plan that will tell you what to do before exercising and what to do if you experience symptoms while exercising.
- If directed by your asthma action plan, always use your pre-exercise asthma medicine (most commonly, inhaled bronchodilators) before beginning exercise.
- Warm-up exercises should be performed, followed by a good cool-down period.
- If the weather is cold, exercise inside or cover your nose and mouth with a mask or scarf.
- If you suffer from allergic asthma, avoid exercising outside when air pollution levels are high.
- When you have a viral infection, such as a cold, limit your physical activity.
- Exercise at your own pace.

Staying active is beneficial to both your physical and mental health. Remember that asthma is not an excuse to avoid exercise. You should be able to enjoy the benefits of an exercise program without experiencing asthma symptoms if you have a proper diagnosis and the most effective treatment.

Adults should engage in at least 150 minutes per week of moderate-intensity aerobic activity, 75 minutes of vigorous aerobic activity, or a combination of the two, according to the American College of Sports Medicine and the Centers for Disease Control and Prevention. They also recommend muscle-strengthening twice a week. To design and implement a safe, effective, and enjoyable program, use the FITT principle. F stands for frequency, I stands for intensity, T stands for time, and T stands for type.

Aerobic Exercise Programs

- Frequency – Be active on at least three to four days per week. Work as many as five days per week.
- Intensity – Intensity refers to the pace of your workout. It is best to keep the intensity low to moderate at first.
- Time – Work out for 30-60 minutes per day. You can do everything at once or divide it into several sessions of at least 10 minutes each.
- Type – Perform rhythmic exercises involving large muscle groups. Brisk walking, cycling, and swimming are all good options. Select activities that you enjoy.

Precautions for Aerobic Exercise

- Exercise should be avoided during the coldest times of the day (early morning or late evening). Also, avoid exercising when pollution or allergen levels are high. Instead, work out inside. There may also be irritants such as smoke or allergens.
- Warm up for 10 minutes before beginning your workout. This can reduce the duration and severity of an attack while exercising and afterward.
- Rest for 10 minutes after your workout.
- If you have been inactive for an extended period, begin with short sessions (10 to 15 minutes). Increase the length of each session by five minutes every two to four weeks. Gradually increase your activity to at least 30 minutes per day on most days of the week.
- Stay hydrated before, during, and after exercise.

- Do not exercise at a level that is too strenuous for you. This may result in an attack and a temporary inability to exercise. It also raises the possibility of injury.

Resistance Training Program

Moderate-intensity resistance training appears to improve your ability to function and promote good health. When developing a resistance exercise program, use the FITT principle as well given by the American College of Sports Medicine and the Centers for Disease Control and Prevention.

- Frequency – Perform resistance training at least twice a week. Schedule a day of rest in between sessions.
- Intensity – Exercise at a moderate level of intensity. You've reached moderate intensity if you can lift a weight 10 to 15 times. When you can only lift a weight eight to ten times, you have reached high intensity.
- Time – This will vary depending on how many exercises you perform.
- Type – Work out all major muscle groups with free weights or a machine. There is no difference between these two approaches.

Resistance Exercise Cautions

- When lifting, avoid holding your breath. This can result in significant changes in blood pressure. This modification may increase the likelihood of passing out or developing an irregular heartbeat.
- If you have joint or other health issues, only do one set for all major muscle groups. Begin with 10–15 repetitions. Before adding another set, work up to 15 to

20 repetitions.

Create an exercise program that provides the most benefit while giving the least risk to your health and physical condition. Consider contacting a health and fitness Professional to collaborate with you and your doctor. Together, you can set realistic goals and create a program that is safe, effective, and enjoyable.

Yoga for Asthma

Along with aerobic and resistance exercises keeping yoga as a part of your daily routine can be beneficial as well. Yoga is a movement-based meditation that focuses on mindfulness. It increases flexibility, balance, and breathing control, among other things. Individuals with asthma may benefit from regular practicing yoga by lowering the severity of their symptoms. Although yoga is not recommended as a first-line treatment for asthma, it can be incorporated into a larger treatment strategy. By reducing stress, opening the chest, and encouraging deep breathing, certain yoga poses might help control symptoms.

There is minimal evidence that yoga offers a definite benefit, according to research. Larger reviews and studies are needed to determine whether or not yoga can improve asthma. However, if you've been correctly controlling your asthma, it's not a bad idea to give it a shot. Yoga has been reported to help persons with asthma feel better. Yoga is thought to be beneficial because it improves posture and opens the chest muscles, which allows for improved breathing. It may also help you learn to manage your breathing and reduce stress, which is a significant cause of asthma symptoms.

Breathing exercises

Breathing exercises are meant to assist you in gaining control of your breathing. These strategies, when used appropriately, can help you breathe more effectively.

Pursed-lip breathing-

Shortness of breath can be relieved by using a technique known as pursed-lip breathing. The exercise increases the amount of oxygen in your lungs, slowing your breathing rate.

- Take a seat in a chair. The neck and shoulders should be relaxed.
- To the count of two, slowly inhale through your nose. Maintain a clenched lip as if you're ready to extinguish a candle.
- To the count of four, slowly exhale through your lips. Take a deep breath and expel all of the air from your lungs.
- Repeat until your breathing is normal again.

Diaphragmatic breathing-

When you have asthma, your body has to work harder to breathe. Diaphragmatic breathing reduces effort by opening the airways, strengthening the abdominal muscles, and improving lung and heart function. This exercise could help relieve your asthma symptoms.

- Take a seat or lie down in bed. Put one hand on your belly and feel it move in and out.
- Slowly inhale through your nose. Your stomach should move out, filling with air like a balloon.
- Exhale through pursed lips for two or three times the length of your inhalation. As the air flows out, your stomach should move in.

During this exercise, keep your chest still. You can make a fist with your other hand on your chest.

Buteyko breathing -

Buteyko breathing is a set of exercises that can help improve asthma symptoms. It is not traditionally taught as part of yoga practice. Here's one method for relieving coughing and wheezing.

- Take a deep breath in and hold it for 3 to 5 seconds. Repeat as needed.
- Exhale slowly through your nose.
- With your pointer and thumb, pinch your nose.
- For 3 to 5 seconds, hold your breath.
- 10 seconds of deep breathing If your symptoms persist, repeat the procedure.

Use your rescue inhaler if your symptoms do not improve within 10 minutes or if your asthma symptoms are severe.

Yoga Asanas

Some yoga poses can help relieve asthma symptoms by relaxing the muscles in your chest. For example,

The bridge pose-

The bridge is a traditional yoga pose that opens the chest and promotes deeper breathing.

- Lie down on your back. Put your feet shoulder-width apart and your knees bent. Put your hands on the floor, palms down.
- Inhale deeply and raise your pelvis, keeping your shoulders and head flat. Take several deep breaths.

Cobra Pose-

Cobra Pose stretches your chest muscles in the same way as Bridge Pose does. It also aids in the improvement of blood circulation, which aids in the breathing process.

- Lower your pelvis slowly to the floor.
- Begin on your stomach. Put your hands on the floor beneath your shoulders, fingers spread wide and forward. Straighten your legs behind you and place them hip-width apart.
- Place your pelvis on the floor. Lift your upper body while pressing into your hands and keeping your hips still. Roll your shoulders back and keep your chin parallel to the floor to maintain a long back of the neck. Hold the position for 15 to 30 seconds.
- Return to the starting position by lowering your upper body.

Seated spinal twist-

Try the seated spinal twist to stretch your respiratory muscles. The pose also extends back muscles and relieves torso stress.

- In a chair, sit up straight. Place your feet firmly on the ground.
- Turn your torso to the right while keeping your shoulders parallel. Make a fist on your right thigh. Take 3–5 deep breaths and then pause.
- Return to the starting point. Rep on the other side.

Pranayama for Asthma-

Yoga breathing exercises may also be beneficial. These techniques can be practiced alone or as part of a gentle yoga routine.

A popular yoga technique for stress relief is alternate nostril breathing. It can also help with asthma-related shortness of breath.

Alternate nostril breathing (Anulom-Vilom)-

- Sit on the floor or bed with your legs crossed. Exhale. Put your right thumb against your right nostril. Breathe in through your left nostril.
- Place your right ring finger on your left nostril. Exhale out of your right nostril.
- Close your right nostril with your right thumb after inhaling through it. Exhale out of your left nostril.
- Repeat as needed.

Victorious breathing (Ujjayi Pranayama)-

Victorious breathing is a yoga technique that, when combined with diaphragmatic breathing, may help improve lung function. An audible breath is also used in the technique, which is thought to promote relaxation.

- Sit up straight and cross-legged on the floor.
- Slowly inhale through your nose.
- Exhale slowly through your mouth, making the sound "aah."

As you get the hang of this breath, try exhaling loudly with your lips closed. Exhale through your nose, followed by an audible breath from the back of your throat.

Asthmatics may benefit from the yoga poses and breathing techniques mentioned above. They may help to open the chest, encourage deep breathing, and control breathing. Although the following poses are appropriate for beginners, individuals should consider their current fitness level as well as any existing injuries before beginning any new exercise program.

To sum up, every individual who has asthma can play, do competitive sports and perform other physical activities with little care and proper medication. Athletes like Jerome Bettis, Amy Van Dyken, Dennis Rodman, David Beckham, and legendary tennis player Novak Djokovic have had asthma. They learned that if they could keep it under control, they could not only continue to participate in sports but also achieve amazing things. There are many more like them. So, if they can do it, you can too.

EIGHT

MYTH -8- TARGETED FAT LOSS OR SPOT REDUCTION IS POSSIBLE

Spot reduction, also known as targeted fat loss, is the idea that fat in a specific location of the body may be targeted by exercising specific muscles in that area. For instance, exercising the abdominal muscles to lose fat in or around the midsection. For some time, the theory of spot reduction has been promoted in the health and fitness world. However, there is little evidence to back it up. Spot reduction is a type of targeted exercise that is designed to burn fat in specific areas of the body. Exercising the triceps to get rid of excess fat on the back of the arms is an example of spot reduction. This popular theory of focusing on specific body parts has led many people to focus only on troublesome areas rather than exercising their entire body. Burning fat with this method may be especially appealing to those who have previously struggled to lose weight or have not achieved the desired results with other methods. But you are going to be disappointed knowing that despite some exceptional case studies, the majority of scientific evidence indicates that it is not possible to lose fat in a single body part by exercising that body part alone. Targeted fat loss or spot reduction is a myth. Your body burns fat based on overall fitness rather than isolated muscle fatigue. It's crucial to understand how the body burns fat to understand why spot reduction may not be effective.

Body Energy System

Every cell in your body requires energy to function, whether it is for muscle contractions for movement and exercise, body temperature regulation, sleep, breathing, or any other bodily function. Knowing more about the fundamentals of human energy processes can help you make better training and dietary choices. the three major energy systems of the body are ATP-PC (The Phosphagen System), Glycolytic (Anaerobic system), and Oxidative (Aerobic System). Now let's try to understand how the body gets the energy?

It is common knowledge that the energy used by the human body each day is derived from the food we eat. But what happens after we eat our meal to convert it into something that the countless individual cells that make up our bodies can use is less well understood.

The simplest and most useful way to think about what happens is as follows: After we consume our meals, the solids and liquids in the foods are digested and broken down into macronutrients, which are the nutritional building blocks of carbohydrates, protein, and fats. The body further processes these into simple compounds that store energy to be used. These compounds are, in broad terms, glucose (from carbohydrates), amino acids (from protein), and fatty acids (from fats). Following digestion, all of these are absorbed into the bloodstream and transported to various cells throughout the body or stored for later use.Inside your cells, those broken-down chemicals from the foods you ate are converted into molecules of adenosine triphosphate, or "ATP" as it's usually known. Consider the ATP molecules to be your fuel. It's immediately useful in this state, as the human body's most easily available source of energy. Although the body stores a small amount of ATP in the muscles, the most is produced by the foods we eat, which is why eating a healthy, well-balanced diet is so vital.

During physical activity, three distinct processes collaborate to split ATP molecules, releasing energy for muscle contraction, force production, and, ultimately, sporting or fitness performance. These processes, or energy systems as they are more commonly known, function as pathways to produce energy, and the intensity and duration of the physical activity we are engaging in determine which pathway serves as the primary fuel source. As soon as you begin exercising, the small amount of ATP stored in our body is depleted and must be replenished in order to continue. This is where the body's three distinct systems come into play, ensuring a constant supply of energy. Different sporting situations require different amounts of energy. In some cases, such as HIIT, energy must be supplied very quickly, whereas, in others, energy must be supplied steadily over a longer period of time rather than at such a high rate. During exercise, all three energy systems are always active; however, the method you rely on most to produce that energy depends on the activity, or more specifically, its intensity and duration. Understanding those energy systems and applying that knowledge to your fitness routine can help you advance your training and improve your results.

The human body's three major energy systems

1. ATP-PC System (The Phosphagen System)

To resynthesize ATP, the ATP-PC system uses a stored molecule in the muscle called creatine phosphate (CP). The energy required to re-join the ADP and free phosphate to form ATP is released by the breakdown of this molecule. This system is anaerobic because it operates without the use of oxygen and produces no waste. This system gives us instant energy, but it is very limited and can only last about 10-12 seconds. As a result, it is used for activities that require short bursts of energy, such as the 100m sprint, long jump, high jump, shot put, and javelin. If you exercise in repeated, brief, maximal, high-intensity bursts (for example, weightlifting, short sprints, or throwing a ball), it will be the dominant energy system for the duration of your workout, but only if you allow enough rest between cycles to replenish the stores.

2. The Glycolytic System (Anaerobic Lactic Energy System)

Glycolysis is simply the breakdown (lysis) of glucose and is made up of a series of chemical reactions that are regulated by enzymes. The anaerobic glycolytic system generates a significant amount of power, but not as quickly or as efficiently as the ATP-PC system. However, it has more fuel supplies and does not burn through all of its fuel as quickly as the ATP-PC system, so it does not fatigue as quickly. After the first ten seconds of intense exercise, the contribution of the fast glycolytic system to energy production increases rapidly. This is accompanied by a decrease in power output as the readily available phosphagens, ATP, and PC begin to deplete. The majority of energy comes from the anaerobic glycolytic system after about 30 seconds of sustained activity. There is a second drop in power output after 45 seconds of sustained intense activity. As the anaerobic glycolytic system begins to fatigue, exercise beyond this point becomes increasingly dependent on the aerobic energy system.

3. The Oxidative System (Aerobic System)

The third and final energy system at work is the oxidative system, also known as the aerobic energy system. Because carbohydrates and fats are only burned in the presence of oxygen, this pathway requires oxygen to produce ATP. While it is not the primary source of ATP at the start of exercise, it can produce a large amount of it, making this system ideal for long-duration, low-intensity cardiovascular activities. This aerobic energy system requires oxygen to function, or else the entire process will slow down and possibly stop. Although you may be burning mostly fat in this energy system, a steady supply of carbohydrates is still required for the breakdown of fat into an energy source. The ratio of fat to carbohydrates used is determined by the intensity and duration of the exercise, as well as the individual's aerobic training experience.

Shorter, more intense workouts, for example, tend to burn more carbohydrates for fuel, whereas longer, less intense workouts burn a higher ratio of fats. The more an individual exercises aerobically, the better their body will be able to use fat as fuel at a given intensity.

It's necessary to keep in mind that all three of these systems help the body meet its energy needs during physical activity. They don't function independently; instead, they take lead at different periods, depending on the duration and intensity of the activity.

Losing body fat can be a difficult task that requires a lot of effort, patience, and dedication. Although many fad diets and fat-burning supplements promise quick results, the most effective way to achieve and maintain a healthy weight is to change your diet, lifestyle, and exercise routine. Furthermore, you can take a few simple steps to promote long-term, sustainable fat loss while also improving your overall health. Knowing how your body uses calories for fuel can help you approach weight loss. Fat, carbohydrates, and protein provide energy. Which one your body uses for energy depends on the activity. Working out at a lesser intensity can be beneficial, but it won't necessarily result in more fat being burned off your body. Exercise at higher intensities and sticking to a calorie deficit diet plan are two ways to boost your calorie burn. Here below are some other ways to increase fat loss.

Strength training for fat loss

Strength training has several health benefits, particularly when it comes to fat loss, according to research. Lifting weights, doing bodyweight exercises, and using gym equipment are all simple ways to begin strength training. Resistance exercise for at least 4 weeks may help reduce body fat by an average of 1.46 percent, according to a study. It may also help you lose body fat mass and visceral fat, which is fat that surrounds your organs in your abdomen.

Consume whole grains instead of refined carbs

Reducing your intake of refined carbohydrates may aid in the loss of excess body fat. Refined grains are removed from their bran and germ during processing, resulting in a low-fiber, low-nutrient final product. Refined carbohydrates also have a high glycemic index (GI), which can produce blood sugar rises and falls, leading to increased hunger. Still, if you eat refined carbs as part of your diet, you're more likely to see these consequences. For long-term, sustainable fat loss, pick nutrient-dense whole grains instead of refined carbs, which are low in fiber and minerals.

Regular Cardio

Cardio, also known as aerobic exercise, is a popular type of exercise. It refers to any form of exercise that specifically targets the heart and lungs. Including cardio in your workout routine could be one of the most effective ways to boost fat burning and weight loss. The majority of research suggests 150–300 minutes of moderate to vigorous exercise per week, or 20–40 minutes of cardio per day.

Eat more fiber

Soluble fibre, which is found in plant foods, absorbs water and moves slowly through your digestive tract, allowing you to feel fuller for longer. Increasing your intake of high-fiber foods may protect against weight gain, according to some studies. Fruits, vegetables, legumes, whole grains, nuts, and seeds are examples of these foods.

Intermittent fasting

Intermittent fasting is a diet pattern that alternates between eating and fasting periods. Although it may not be suitable for everyone, some research suggests that it may help with both weight loss and fat loss. One intermittent fasting review looked at alternate-day fasting, which is a method in which you alternate between days of fasting and eating normally. This method reduced body weight by up to 7% and body fat by up to 5.5 kg over 3–12 weeks.

Another small study found that when combined with resistance training, eating only during an 8-hour window each day helped reduce fat mass while maintaining muscle mass.

There are various types of intermittent fasting, such as Eat Stop Eat, the Warrior Diet, the 16/8 method, and the 5:2 diet. Find a variation that works for your schedule, and don't be afraid to experiment to find out what works best for you.

To lose body fat in a healthy way, avoid crash diets and dangerous supplements. Rather, incorporate healthy habits into your routine, such as eating whole grains instead of refined carbs, substituting water for sugary drinks, trying probiotics, or drinking coffee. To promote long-term, sustainable fat burning, combine these simple nutrition tips with a well-rounded diet and an active lifestyle.

Along with the right diet plans and the right exercise schedule and the above-mentioned points, it is most important to understand for increasing the fat loss one has to maintain a calorie deficit plan. Let's try to understand what is calorie deficit and how it works.

What Exactly Is a Calorie?

A calorie is a type of energy unit. It is the amount of heat required to raise the temperature of one gram of water by one degree Celsius. Calories in food provide energy in the form of heat, allowing our bodies to function even when they are at rest. Your total daily energy expenditure, or TDEE, is the total number of calories you burn per day. When TDEE is calculated, it includes calories burned during exercise and non-exercise movement, the number of calories burned during digestion which is known as the thermic effect of food, or TEF, and calories used to maintain vital bodily functions such as breathing and blood circulation.

What Is a Calorie Deficit?

When you consume fewer calories than you burn, you create a calorie deficit. Because calories are a unit of heat or energy, this is also known as an energy deficit. A caloric deficit, regardless of the terminology, is required for weight loss. It should be noted, however, that not all nutrition experts or researchers agree that losing excess weight is as simple as reducing calorie intake. The sections that follow will explain calorie deficits and how to maintain realistic weight loss expectations while reducing your food intake.

A calorie deficit occurs when you consume fewer calories than your body requires to perform all of its essential functions. For example, if you burn 2,000 calories today but only consume 1,800, you have a 200-calorie deficit. When there is a calorie deficit, your body obtains energy or fuel from stored fat. In this case, stored fat is equivalent to stored energy. Instead of using energy from food, your body can use it to keep moving. You lose weight when your body burns fat for energy.

There are differing views on calorie deficits and how they contribute to healthy and sustainable weight loss. According to some nutrition-based organizations, a calorie deficit of 3500 calories per week is required to lose one pound of bodyweight. To achieve this goal, the National Institute of Health recommends cutting 500 calories per day. According to research, the concept of 3500 calories per pound of bodyweight dates back to the 1950s, when Max Wishnofsky, a New York doctor, stated it in a report. Many top health officials and agencies have affirmed this statement since then.

You may have experienced these effects if you've tried to lose weight by cutting calories. Many opposers of this ideology, however, argue that losing weight is not as simple as creating a specific calorie deficit. When you cut calories, your body has several mechanisms in place to keep you from losing weight. Your metabolism slows, hormone levels shift, hunger cravings increase, and you may become less active without even realizing it. You might expect linear, consistent weight loss if you create a calorie deficit based on numbers like 3500 calories per pound. However, the human body is complex, and weight loss rarely occurs in a straight line. In other words, even though you continued to consume fewer calories than you expended, your weight loss will begin to slow rather than accelerate. Some dietitians agree, adding that calorie deficits are only one of many factors that influence weight loss, including gender, exercise habits, and others. One thing that scientists appear to agree on is that a calorie deficit can help people lose weight. However, the extent to which it can assist varies depending on several things. When trying to lose weight, keeping this in mind might help you maintain reasonable expectations.

Creating Calorie Deficit

While it may appear to be straightforward to lose weight by creating a calorie deficit, many people struggle with the process because it is not as simple as it appears. The good news is that you don't have to go on a fad diet or juice fast to lose weight. Rather than starvation, creating a calorie deficit for weight loss should be based on increasing your health and wellness.

Portion sizes should be adjusted.

You'll likely consume fewer calories per day naturally if you adjust your portion sizes, improve your snacking habits, and choose nutrient-rich, filling foods at mealtime. When trying to lose weight, it is critical not to eat too little because this can reduce the likelihood of long-term weight loss. Rather than focusing on eliminating foods, focus on increasing your intake of high-volume, nutrient-dense foods.

Stay Physically Active

The number of calories your body requires each day is determined by your level of activity. This includes both your exercise and non-exercise physical movement. A calorie deficit occurs when you increase the number of calories your body requires while maintaining the same number of calories from food. Physical activity has numerous health benefits that go far beyond the effects of potential weight loss. Adding movement that you enjoy to your days can help improve your mental and physical health. Weight loss may occur naturally as a result of your increased activity without you feeling like exercise is just a tool for burning calories. Exercise influences your hunger and appetite. Moderate to vigorous activity can satisfy hunger without increasing the amount of food consumed later in the day. This means that increasing physical activity can increase calorie burn, decrease hunger, and create a natural calorie deficit. Although both calorie deficits and exercise can aid with short-term weight loss, studies have shown that combining the two is the best approach to maintaining weight loss over time.

In conclusion, spot reduction or targeted fat loss is a complete myth, you may be able to tone up the muscle with targeted strength training but the fat loss in a particular body zone is not possible. You will never achieve a flat stomach by performing abdominal exercises alone. This is because a muscle does not own the fat that surrounds it. Sit-ups, for example, will undoubtedly strengthen your abdominal muscles, but they will not remove the layer of fat that covers the muscles. To lose fat anywhere in your body, you must burn calories through a program that includes both cardiovascular and weight training along with calorie deficit. This will reduce fat stores throughout your body, including targeted areas.

Bibliograhraphy

4 Myths about Strength Training for Women. https://www.acefitness.org/resources/pros/expert-articles/5040/4-myths-about-strength-training-for-women/. Accessed 21 June 2022.

"5 Common Myths on Periods You Need To Know About." PharmEasy Blog, 1 Feb. 2022, https://pharmeasy.in/blog/5-common-myths-on-periods-you-need-to-know-about/.

"12 Sustainable Ways to Burn Body Fat." Healthline, 29 Nov. 2021, https://www.healthline.com/nutrition/best-ways-to-burn-fat.

Bender, Dana. The Principles of Strength Training for New Clients - NASM. https://blog.nasm.org/strength-training-new-clients. Accessed 21 June 2022.

"Cardio vs. Weight Lifting: Which Is Better for Weight Loss?" Healthline, 24 Oct. 2017, https://www.healthline.com/nutrition/cardio-vs-weights-for-weight-loss.

David. A Beginner's Guide to Energy Systems in the Human Body. https://www.freeletics.com/en/blog/posts/human-energy-systems-beginners-guide/. Accessed 21 June 2022.

"Does Fat Turn into Muscle?" Healthline, 2 Mar. 2021, https://www.healthline.com/nutrition/does-fat-turn-into-muscle.

Does Lifting Weights Make Women Bulky? | ISSA. https://www.issaonline.com/blog/post/ladies-lifting-heavy-wont-make-you-bulk-up. Accessed 21 June 2022.

Exercise during a Period: Tips, Benefits, and More. 19 Nov. 2021, https://www.medicalnewstoday.com/articles/326364.

"Exercise Is Medicine." Wikipedia, 2 Apr. 2022. Wikipedia, https://en.wikipedia.org/w/

index.php?title=Exercise_is_Medicine&oldid=1080619487.

"Is Height Genetic? Why and Why Not?" Healthline, 11 Dec. 2020, https://www.healthline.com/health/is-height-genetic.

"Is It Possible to Target Fat Loss to Specific Body Parts?" Healthline, 5 Jan. 2018, https://www.healthline.com/nutrition/targeted-weight-loss.

Lewis-McCormick, Irene. A Woman's Guide to Muscle and Strength. Human Kinetics, 2012.

Menato, Francesca. "6 Complete Myths About Strength Training + Weight Lifting For Women." Women's Health, 3 Jan. 2018, http://http://www.womenshealthmag.co.uk/fitness/strength-training/a704005/myths-about-strength-training-and-weight-lifting-debunked/.

"Muscle: Types of Muscles, Functions & Common Conditions." Cleveland Clinic, https://my.clevelandclinic.org/health/body/21887-muscle. Accessed 21 June 2022.

Nam, Paul. Body Transformation: Get Lean Or Bulk Up: For Men & Women. Paul Nam, 2019.

"National Heart, Lung, and Blood Institute." Wikipedia, 23 May 2022. Wikipedia, https://en.wikipedia.org/w/index.php?title=National_Heart,_Lung,_and_Blood_Institute

Parmar, Riddhi. "8 Best Exercises To Do During Periods." PharmEasy Blog, 2 Feb. 2022, https://pharmeasy.in/blog/8-best-exercises-to-do-during-periods/.

"8 Best Exercises To Do During Periods." PharmEasy Blog, 2 Feb. 2022, https://pharmeasy.in/blog/8-best-exercises-to-do-during-periods/.

Schuler, Lou, et al. The New Rules of Lifting for Women: Lift Like a Man, Look Like a Goddess. United States, Penguin Publishing Group, 2008.

Sims, Stacy, and Selene Yeager. ROAR: How to Match Your Food and Fitness to Your Unique Female Physiology for Optimum Performance, Great Health, and a Strong, Lean Body for Life. Harmony/Rodale, 2016.

Statesman Journal. http://www.statesmanjournal.com/story/life/livingwell/2015/12/14/cardio-vs-weights-one-beats-fat-loss/77055976/. Accessed 21 June 2022.

"Types of Body Fat: Benefits, Risks, Diet, Body Fat Percentage & More." Healthline, 24 May 2019, https://www.healthline.com/health/types-of-body-fat.

"Weight Lifting For Children And Teens." Bodybuilding.Com, 6 Mar. 2002, https://www.bodybuilding.com/content/weight-lifting-for-children-and-teens.html.

"Weight Loss vs. Fat Loss: How to Tell the Difference." Healthline, 9 Feb. 2021, https://www.healthline.com/nutrition/weight-loss-vs-fat-loss.

"Weight Training Stunts Growth – An Evidence-Based Myth Buster." Physio Network, 6 Oct. 2018, https://www.physio-network.com/blog/weight-training-stunts-growth-an-evidence-based-myth-buster/.

"What Is a Calorie Deficit?" Verywell Fit, https://www.verywellfit.com/what-is-a-calorie-deficit-3495538. Accessed 21 June 2022.

"Which Foods to Eat and Avoid During Your Period." Flo.Health - #1 Mobile Product for Women's Health, https://flo.health/menstrual-cycle/lifestyle/diet-and-nutrition/foods-to-eat-on-period. Accessed 21 June 2022.

"Will Lifting Weights Stunt Your Growth? | Everything You Need To Know!" Anabolic Aliens, https://anabolicaliens.com/blogs/the-signal/will-lifting-weights-stunt-your-growth. Accessed 21 June 2022.

Yoga for Asthma: How It Helps and Poses to Try. 9 July 2021, https://www.medicalnewstoday.com/articles/asthma-yoga.

"Yoga for Asthmatics: Moves to Try and More." Healthline, 27 Feb. 2020, https://www.healthline.com/health/asthma/yoga-for-asthmatics.

Zarndt, Gabby Landsverk, Jessica. "5 Weight Lifting Myths for Women and the Health Benefits Women Who Lift Weights Gain." Insider, https://www.insider.com/guides/health/fitness/weight-lifting-myths-for-women. Accessed 21 June 2022.

Printed by Libri Plureos GmbH in Hamburg,
Germany